How to Marry
a Mensch*

The Love Coach's Guide
to Meeting Your Mate

How to Marry
a Mensch*

Robin Gorman Newman

FAIR WINDS
PRESS
GLOUCESTER, MASSACHUSETTS

*Mensch: a decent, responsible person even your mother would love

Text © 2006 by Robin Gorman Newman

First published in the USA in 2006 by
Fair Winds Press, a member of
Quayside Publishing Group
33 Commercial Street
Gloucester, MA 01930

10 09 08 07 06   1 2 3 4 5

ISBN 1-59233-167-X

Library of Congress Cataloging-in-Publication Data

Gorman Newman, Robin
How to marry a mensch: the love coach's guide to meeting your mate/
Robin Gorman Newman.

p. cm.
ISBN 1-59233-167-X (pbk.)
1. Dating (Social customs) 2. Mate selection.
3. Single women--Psychology. 4. Jewish women--Psychology. I. Title.
HQ801.G5953 2006
646.7'7089924--dc22

2005028614

Cover illustration by Barbara McGregor/www.artscounselinc.com
Book design by Carol Holtz Design

Printed and bound in USA

For Marc, the mensch in my life, and our
mensch-in-the-making son, Seth

In memory of my beloved mother, Sylvia Gorman

Special thanks to:

Ellen Phillips, for this opportunity
Patty Moosbrugger, for her efforts
Barbara McGregor, for her cover illustration
Aaron Gorman, for being a devoted mensch father
Dorothy and Emily Safron, who I hope will marry mensches
Barbara Gorman Safron, for her sisterly love
Larry Benjamin, for so patiently handling my computer challenges
Richard Arfin, for creating my Web site
Michelle Foglia, for her supportive ear
Meredith Harris, for helping recruit contributors
Michele Laub, for her wise voice
Adrienne Sioux Koopersmith, for her enthusiastic e-mails
The folks at the Great Neck Public Library Lakeville Branch
My true friends, whom I will always treasure . . . you know who you are
My beloved bird, Chiffon, for her spirit and companionship
My love-coaching clients, whose tales are woven into this book

And all those who shared their personal stories and words of wisdom.
I greatly appreciate your candor and participation.

[Contents]

Intro | Meet Your Love Coach

When looking for a job, you might seek the assistance of a recruiter. If you want to get in shape, you might decide to hire a personal trainer. So why is it that when it comes to your love life, often the last thought that comes to mind is to enlist the help of a professional to guide you in the right direction? Maybe it never occurred to you to consult with an expert in the area. Perhaps you didn't know any existed? It's not like you can pick up the Yellow Pages and look under "Love Coach"—though one day that may be a possibility!

When I was single, I would definitely have benefited from consulting a person with the insights I have now, but I wasn't aware of any experts in this area. To my knowledge, coaches (except in sports) unfortunately didn't exist at that time. So you have an edge now that I didn't during my struggle with singlehood. You will gain from the wisdom of The Love Coach, and by reading this book, you are taking a proactive step toward creating a more satisfying social life.

What *Is* a Love Coach?

What does a love coach do, anyway? I serve as a guide to help you navigate and deal with the ever-changing social scene—one that has grown increasingly complex due to the advent of the Internet. This book is your personal introduction to love coaching, and will provide advice that you can follow on your own. Most chapters have one or more exercises for you to spend time on, as well as useful advice, connections, and stories of my clients' experiences that you can relate to and benefit from.

I am not a therapist or a matchmaker. If I were to do a phone consult or meet with you personally, I would assess your situation through in-depth discussion and leave you with a detailed plan of action that you could follow to improve your social life. I would tell you specifically where to go and what to do to meet the right people, and discuss any relationship issues that might arise. I would develop a plan for your love life, which you will ultimately learn to create for yourself through this book.

Once you have made up your mind that meeting a mate is a top priority, frustration often follows because the actual encounter—when and how it will happen—is beyond your control. It's easy to wish you had a crystal ball, but unless you consult a gifted psychic (and believe in the advice), you have to accept the unknown. However, there is much you *can* control through your actions and attitude, and that is what I will address.

How I Became The Love Coach

My work as The Love Coach started after the publication of two editions of my first book, *How to Meet a Mensch in New York.* In case you're not aware, a *mensch* is defined, on the most basic level, as a decent, responsible person. I was on the lecture circuit, meeting many singles, when I first became aware that people crave personal advice. I could deliver the most dynamic, idea-inspiring lecture, but in the end, no two people have exactly the same issues or concerns.

At the suggestion of a friend who was single, I decided to let people know of my availability for private consultations, and the rest is history. Largely through word of mouth, I have since worked with hundreds of singles nationwide, both men and women, of all ages and backgrounds, and it has been immensely gratifying to make a difference in people's lives. I want to do the same for you. Reading this book is a positive step in the right direction.

Believe me, I've been there. When I was single, it felt like I would never meet Mr. Right Mensch (MRM), yet now I am a married woman—a Mrs. Mensch. Better yet, I am a married woman with loads of advice to share, based on my own experience, my research, and hundreds of client consultations that will hopefully both inspire and lead you to the kind of social life you have always wanted.

Since you may not be in a position to contact me, think of me as your personal love coach as you read the stories in this book. I will attempt to lead you strategically down the path (or aisle) to meet your mensch. While there is no quick fix or "cure-all pill" for romance, the mere fact that you are seeking advice is a leap of faith toward your love goal. In fact, in my love-coaching practice, several times I've found that once people made an appointment to consult with me, they would meet someone interesting to date just prior to our appointment.

Why should that be? Because they put themselves in the right mind-set and established their social life as a priority. That's what you need to do. Taking the initiative is often half the battle—so you're on your way. You might also visit my Web site, www.lovecoach.com, for some ongoing inspiration.

Read on!

Robin Gorman Newman
The Love Coach

(Note: Many of the names of the people whose stories I share in this book have been changed to protect their privacy.)

Chapter 1 | *I was in your shoes:*

CONFESSIONS OF A FORMERLY SINGLE WOMAN TURNED LOVE COACH

If I had been told when I was single that one day I'd be writing this book, I'd have said that was crazy. Never in my wildest dreams did I imagine that one day I'd be considered a relationship expert worthy of dishing out advice to hundreds of singles—and now you. Yet here I am, The Love Coach, a "survivor" of the scene, so to speak, and I'm ready to share. But it wasn't easy getting to this point.

What I Wish I Knew When I Was Single

When I graduated from college and joined the workforce, I often felt like I had a second job just because I was single. By day I worked in public relations, and by night I was searching, hoping to find that elusive someone. I spent many an evening disappointed or waiting, hopeful that I would hear from a prospective date. Can you relate?

On those nights I chose to stay home, I often spent hours combing through magazines and singles literature from the multitude of organizations that placed me on their mailing lists. My mission was to plot out a social agenda for the weekend, but not just for myself. I was a virtual one-woman singles clearinghouse for the lovelorn in my social circle, and there were many of us. All my friends knew whom to call to find out the hottest events to attend so they, too, could attempt to meet someone. It often felt so overwhelming . . . so exhausting . . . so expensive . . . so endless. I was on the dating warpath big-time, and in my mind, the more frequently I went out, the faster I would meet my Mr. Right Mensch. Boy, was that wrong! What I actually wound up doing was spinning my wheels (and wearing out my soles and my soul) in a driven attempt to become part of a couple.

> Mensch: A decent, responsible person even your mother would love.

Leaving No Stone Unturned

I had friends who met their mate in the office, but I always worked in female-dominated departments or very small companies, so that didn't work for me. As an active single, I left few stones unturned in my quest for a mensch. I pounded the pavement, trying everything from personal ads to happy-hour mixers to volunteer work to organized tours to tennis leagues to golf camp (I had never played in my life). I was a woman on the go, but I was so on the socializing track that at times I made myself crazy trying to cover as many bases as possible.

I never had many fix-ups, and those I did have didn't work. I quickly grew tired of singles dances—it felt like I saw a lot of the same faces over and over again. Tennis lessons were great for my backhand, but that's about it: I never had a love match. Weekend getaways were fun, but I spent more time packing than connecting. Volunteer work warmed my heart, but being a generally over-whelmed and overworked New Yorker, my schedule never permitted much in this area.

I kept myself busy, and time passed quickly, but a long-term romance eluded me. I did date a couple of guys, in particular, who I thought had potential, but neither worked out. The first broke up with me for someone else, and on the rebound from him, I met a new guy, but I was still hung up and brokenhearted from the first breakup. I suppose if the new guy had been "the one," it would eventually have worked out anyway, but I know I had my hesitations.

Does all this sound familiar to you? Do you feel as if you're making great effort to circulate and it's just not paying off? Have you had relationships that led nowhere? Do you question the choices you're making and wonder why you haven't met a commit-ment-minded mensch? When was the last time you went out? Have you ever actually dated a mensch?

On the Wrong Track

Now that I am removed from the "scene" and can look back on my endeavors, I have reached the conclusion that my approach was not altogether strategic. While my intentions were good, I might have made my life easier if I had devised a game plan or plan of action to help accomplish my socializing goals. Yes—a plan, some direction, and a greater assessment of what was truly important to me.

But I'm not sure that I even knew myself well enough to really identify what I needed and expected from a mate. I have always marveled at couples who marry young (in my book, that's under the age of thirty). I find it amazing that they can be so sure of what will make them happy—either that or they're just willing to take the leap. Some of the stories that I share later on will prove that you can find true love at any age.

[*You can find true love at any age.*]

I Met a Mensch, and Now This Book Will Help You Meet Yours

I met my husband when I was just turning thirty. Not that I was old, but as I reached what I considered a milestone in my life—a new decade of maturity—I felt like I had waited forever to find the right person.

To hear my close friend Donna tell it, back in my single days, we had many a conversation where I said that I couldn't fathom how I would ever meet a man to marry. I didn't want just any man, but the right one—a mensch—the person I was meant to be with. You might call it a soul mate. I refer to it as my *beshert*, which means "the one you're fated to be with."

"What would it take? When would the day come? Where were the men we had both been waiting for?" I would ask Donna. It felt like we'd both been dating forever, and we were getting burned out. We spent hours discussing it over the phone in chats that often lasted until 2:00 a.m., and our mutual questions and romantic insecurities were not resolved until years later.

Fortunately, both of our stories have happy endings. Donna's search ended happily, but later than mine. I met my husband on an organized singles trip to London and Paris. It's a funny story that I often tell when I give a talk, so I'd like to share it with you.

From Rock to Romance: Robin's Story

I was working at a public relations firm at the time and had a client who was a young, single, gorgeous (my ideal physical type—yours, too, I'll bet) rock-concert producer. I had never met anyone like him in all my socializing years, and I was smitten. Tall and dark, with piercing blue eyes and a "no need for tooth whitener" smile, he was exciting, edgy, eligible, but off-limits.

Dating a client was taboo at my company (and he never asked me out, anyway), but we became fast friends and often spent time together shooting the breeze after hours over coffee or drinks or on the phone. I was supposed to travel with him and his business partners to Estonia in the Baltics to promote the rock concert they were staging there, but at the last minute, all the plans were canceled due to lack of funding from potential corporate sponsors.

Now not only did I not have any vacation plans, but my dreams of a clandestine romantic rendezvous in the faraway Baltics were quashed. While I was really disappointed, I decided to seize the moment and look for another way to make the most of my allotted vacation time. After doing loads of research, I turned up a singles trip with a group I knew little about.

While I wasn't sure what to make of them, the timing of the trip was right on the mark for me, and I said to myself, "What's the worst? If I hate it, I'll hop onto an early flight home." It was certainly better than staying home, wallowing in disappointment and pining over the rock-concert producer. But, as luck would have it, and as you can probably guess, it was on this trip that I met my husband. Who would have thought?

So you see, good can most definitely come from what seems bad or uncertain at the time. Had I gone off to Estonia with the hunky rock-concert producer, chances are that nothing remotely romantic would have happened except in my dreams, and instead,

I met the man who became my husband.

What struck me as funny when I met him was that I had been hearing for years from various sources, "You will meet someone when you least expect it." And my constant reply was, "But I always least expect it . . . so when . . . how?" Oddly enough, the reality is, I did meet my husband when it was the last thing on my mind— and maybe that's why it happened.

Yes, I was on a singles trip, so I put myself in a situation that was promising, but I actually wasn't completely open to meeting someone. Since I was upset about the concert's falling through, I had the rock-concert producer on my mind and wasn't looking for anyone else at that moment. In fact, I was quite preoccupied handpicking postcards and purchasing T-shirts to send him back home.

Luckily for me, the European tour I was on lasted two weeks, and it gave me a chance to gradually get to know Marc, my future husband. It's not that I wasn't interested in him initially. I actually found him attractive and kind, but I wasn't quite ready to give someone else a chance.

Marc tells a funny story about a Creamsicle he bought from an ice-cream cart on a hot day in London that he tried to get me to eat. He thought it was the true act of being a mensch, offering a cool sweet to take some of the edge off the stifling temperature. London was having an unusual heat wave, and ice cubes were a rare commodity, it seemed, so ice cream was the next best thing. While I appreciated the gesture, I do not like Creamsicles (I'm a chocolate gal by choice). Even though I gracefully declined, Marc took my rejection of his offer as lack of interest in him. This was totally not true, and gradually he came to know that.

As the trip went on, I slowly realized that I was hanging on to a pipe dream with the rock-concert producer, and here, in lively

London and picturesque (not to mention blissfully romantic) Paris, was a man who was attainable, appealing, and, better yet, interested in me. Plus, he caught my eye as well. So, I thought, why not give it a shot?!

The moral of the story is that you must have hope. You can never know when a decision you make will alter your life forever . . . and potentially for the better. Just when it seems like Mr. Right Mensch is nowhere in sight, he may emerge—and to your surprise and delight, you might learn that he has been searching for you as well. But you have to be in the mensch-hunting game to win at it.

Getting Personal: Donna's Story

In case you're wondering how Donna ultimately met her husband, it was through a personal ad I wrote for her. Donna is a beautiful woman but was in a socializing rut. She lived in a suburban town and kept going to bars and clubs because she liked to dance and didn't know what else to do, beyond work, to get out of the house. Sure, she'd meet men, but the men she met were the ones who were confident enough to approach her. Often they were cocky types, because they weren't intimidated by her striking looks.

Shy men didn't know what to say to Donna. She didn't come across very approachable, because she herself was shy and pretty— a tricky combination when you meet someone for the first time. She seemed like a snob, which was as far from the truth as you could imagine. Not having much self-confidence, despite her looks, she made the wrong choices in men.

Donna also readily gave out her phone number, because she was flattered just to have been asked, without giving any real thought to the type of guy who asked for it. Was it someone she'd even want to date? Did she know anything about him? Okay, sometimes it's hard to know based on the first encounter, but you

CHAPTER 1 | I WAS IN YOUR SHOES

have to ask yourself: If you've been dating a lot of the wrong types, is there something wrong with your selection process? Are you selling yourself short and don't realize it until you get hurt?

One night, Donna and I went out for dinner, and she shared her frustration about the challenges of meeting desirable men. It was evident to me that she needed to shake up her routine. While it was hard for her to envision, she needed to take some risks and venture in new directions. I suggested she take a class or join a volleyball league, but neither appealed to her.

When I proposed she write a personal ad, she turned up her nose. She was afraid of the type of people who might respond to an ad. Would they be desperate? Schleps? Gonifs (thieves)? Illegal immigrants? You name it, the crazy thoughts crossed her mind. There was no rational basis for her fear, because, if you think about it, she hadn't been meeting great guys at clubs, so in a sense, how much worse could this approach be?

Donna agreed, and admitted it had to do with her own insecurity and perception of personal ads. To her, people place ads because they can't meet someone face-to-face. Nobody wants them. They're not presentable. They are rejects, willing to try anything to connect with a potential mate. Not that she saw herself as a reject, but again, this wasn't coming from a rational place. When you're fearful, it's hard to think straight.

Donna was surprised by her own lack of success with men and never anticipated the need to take the type of action that placing a personal ad represented to her. We talked it out, and I explained that I didn't see it as an act of desperation but, rather, the sign of someone's wanting to take destiny into her own hands by opening up a new world of socializing opportunity.

To me, that was smart, and not in any way indicative of a weakness on somebody's part. A weakness in this case would be

21

an unwillingness to try, and an inability to give someone the benefit of the doubt in terms of his motivation to respond to her ad or place his own. Since Donna didn't buy into my philosophy right away, to spur her into action, I volunteered to write the ad for her, and then she became a bit more open-minded. I actually went so far as to place it for her initially, since I wasn't convinced she would follow through. Eventually, Donna caught on and wound up running the ad in various daily and weekly newspapers.

A KERNEL OF ROMANCE (HOLD THE BUTTER): THERESA AND BRAD

Theresa and Brad have a funny story from their courtship days. They were fixed up by a mutual friend, John, who suggested a bunch of them go to a ball game one night after work. Theresa sat next to Brad at the stadium. They talked, but conversation wasn't overly flowing. Brad was quite taken by the game and focused most of his attention on it. He'd get quite enthused when a hit was made, sometimes shouting out to the crowd and standing up and cheering.

Theresa didn't know what to make of him. She could see he had tremendous enthusiasm for the sport, but what about an interest in her? She thought he was attractive and knew from what their friend had said that he was very smart. That appealed to her; but, since they didn't talk much during the game, she couldn't reach any concrete conclusion on her own.

As the evening moved on, Brad bought himself a tub of popcorn and offered some to Theresa. Next thing Theresa knew, Brad spilled a bit of the popcorn on his lap. (Thankfully, it didn't have butter.) Noticing it, and since Brad seemed oblivious, Theresa quickly brushed it off his lap. He thanked her, and they continued watching the game. Theresa looked down at Brad's lap again a few minutes later and saw more popcorn, so she did the same.

Ultimately, Donna met her future husband when he responded to her ad, but it did take about six months before they connected. For a while, I helped her review some of the responses so she could decide whom to go out with. Most left voice-mail messages, but some wrote letters and sent photos. It was a process that was new and somewhat daunting to her, so enlisting my help made it more palatable for her—and more gratifying for me. It actually became a fun way for us to hang out after work.

This time, Brad didn't say anything, since someone had just hit a home run, and he was busy cheering.

A few more minutes passed and Theresa noticed that Brad had spilled half the tub of popcorn on his lap. She glanced over and saw that he was giggling. This time, Brad looked at her, and they both laughed. It was clear to Theresa that Brad was flirting with her. Maybe not the first time he dropped some of the popcorn, but certainly the second and third times.

Theresa thought it was funny, and found Brad's sense of humor really adorable. They wound up dating, and are now married with two children.

MORAL OF THE STORY
A little popcorn can go a long way. There are lots of ways to express to someone that you're interested. If you are shy, you may have to be a little more creative, as in the case of Brad. While he wasn't one for words, he let his actions do the talking, and really endeared himself to Theresa. She thought he was a person who knew how to have fun. While he tends to be more on the serious side by nature, he doe have moments of letting loose and laughing. What could be more appealing than a mensch who is smart and playful?

Today, both Donna and her mensch husband admit that had it not been for the ad, they never would have met. They lived in different towns and never socialized in the same places. In fact, he disliked bars and clubs, so even if they had lived in the same town, he would not have been frequenting those places.

The key for Donna, and for many, was to learn how to *act* like she wanted to get married and not just *say* it or *think* it. I will address this notion again in Chapter 2. It's a critical piece of advice that can totally transform your social life. Once Donna got serious about her pursuit of a mensch and followed my advice, her love life took shape. It happened over time—but then, anything good is worth waiting for, as long as it doesn't take a lifetime. Donna and her husband now live in the suburbs of New York with their two young children, and she happily recalls the story of what brought them together. I'm delighted to have played a part in it.

Be Socially Strategic

Let Donna be your inspiration. You can find *your* Mr. Right Mensch, too, if you believe it and act on it. My goal in writing this book is to empower you to be proactive, and focus your social efforts in directions that can potentially be the most fruitful during your mensch quest. That's what it's all about— cutting to the chase—weeding through the "meet" market—having direction. You need to be socially strategic and create a plan.

Strategy? A plan? You probably never thought about your social life in those terms, but that may be exactly what is holding you back. Before you venture out into unknown social territory, it is essential to think about what activities you are pursuing and why. Ask yourself these questions, and answer as honestly as possible:

- Are you just doing what is convenient and familiar, but isn't working for you?

- Are you going along with the direction and desires of friends, but not having a stitch of fun in the process?
- Are you filling your free time with activities to pass the hours and days, but not to enhance your life or allow you to potentially connect with someone new?
- Do you listen to the dating frustrations of friends, and, as you give advice to them, become aware that you are socially challenged as well?
- Are you living at home with your folks, yet dreaming of a life of independence and creating your own family? Does it seems beyond your grasp?
- When you think ahead to the next five to ten years, do you envision that you'll likely be in the same place in your life? And if so, how does that feel?
- Do you need to break old patterns and try something you never thought you would enjoy?
- Would you benefit from taking a socializing hiatus to rejuvenate yourself?

These are some tough questions, but I urge you to answer them. Believe me when I say that you are not alone in the challenge of meeting your *mensch*. But I am firmly convinced that there is someone for everyone, as long as you make a genuine effort.

Many people invest so much time in their careers that their social lives often take a back seat. Before you know it, the years move on, and you wonder how you reached your current stage in life. Did you ever think that at this time you would be without a mate? This holds true whether you've never married or you're divorced or widowed. You might be single for different reasons, but the bottom line is, there is more you could be doing. Your resume may be impressive, but you haven't had a great date in ages and don't know what is wrong.

If this is a sentiment you share, then you are the typical person I have worked with as The Love Coach. Men and women of all ages come to see me because they either don't know where to begin to socialize or they recognize that their efforts need some fine-tuning. The options seem countless, and they can't focus their energy. They might also need an attitude check or some ego boosting if it feels like they're in a dating slump.

LESSONS FROM THE LOVE COACH

Acting like you want to get married means being open-minded, trying new things, going out at least once a week to socialize, taking chances, talking to people, dating only available men, etc. If you are able to identify what may be holding you back in conquering the social scene, it will make the effort you expend more worthwhile.

Reorder Your Priorities

It's not uncommon to feel stuck, but once you get started again, things will start to flow. You just have to take the leap and make a commitment to establish socializing as a priority and, if need be, reach out for suggestions and motivation from a coach.

You need to give yourself permission to spend the time that is necessary to make good things result in the romance department. It won't happen unless you sincerely exert the effort. If that means leaving the office a bit earlier a couple of times a week so you can go out on a Thursday, a popular night to socialize, can you allow yourself to do that? If it means getting to work a bit earlier in the morning, isn't it worth it? If it means shopping less and saving so you can spend money on a singles trip or a fund-raising event, will you do it?

If most of your weekend activity is hanging with married friends with children, would you be willing to give that up to schedule new pursuits that could be social? Your married friends would be likely to understand, and even support your efforts, because they'd want you to be happy. But it is certainly easier to be with friends, because you can rationalize it by saying. "Well, at least I know I'll have a good time."

Some clients I've worked with tell me that they try very hard to meet people, yet often, when I ask what they are pursuing, they can't readily think of anything. That's because in their head and heart they feel like they are making a great effort since they know they want it more than anything and think about it constantly. However, there's a big difference between *saying* you want to get married and *acting* like it. I can't emphasize this point enough!

There needs to be a correlation between perception and reality, and you must realistically assess your efforts. How often are you

WORDS OF WISDOM

Rosemary Martino Chaifetz, married twenty-three years: "One should marry a mensch because not to leads to heartache and bitterness, and who wants that? If you are looking for a mensch, don't confuse lust with love. Look for the one who laughs easily, engages in good conversation, reads widely, and has integrity. Look for the one who would make not only a loyal friend and lover but an excellent parent. Also, you need not only to be compatible with the positive aspects of a person but to be tolerant of the negative. If you can live with them, and even embrace some of them, you're in good shape."

going out? Do you talk to people when you go out? Are you open-minded when you meet someone new? Are you always going to the same places unsuccessfully? Do you date emotionally unavailable men?

At least in the beginning, it may help to keep a Socializing Notebook and record your pursuits. (See next page, "Create a Socializing Notebook," for more on this.) Review it at the end of the month and see if you're convinced that you truly made an honest attempt.

Of course, it takes time, patience, and energy, but with the right direction and attitude, you can achieve your romantic goals, much like anything you aspire to in life. Remember to endeavor to keep socializing high on your "To Do" list. It's easy for it to take a backseat once life and other responsibilities set in, but try to fight that temptation. Focus on creating a manageable plan for yourself, and keep it up!

EXERCISE:
Create a Socializing Notebook

- Create a Love Log or Socializing Notebook to track your mensch-meeting efforts. It can be as simple as a spiral-bound notebook or something with a pretty cover or colored paper that will inspire you to write. By keeping all your notes and reflections in one place, you can refer to them over time and get a better sense of your feelings, efforts, and challenges, much like a diary. You can even take it with you on the train or bus and write when the spirit moves you.

- Use it to record both your successes and your disappointments, so you can learn what worked for you and also learn from your mistakes and not repeat them. At the top of the first page, write "Socializing" in indelible red ink. Do the same on your daily To Do list (if you have one), and keep "Socializing" at the top of the list.

- Schedule time every week for socializing. Put it in your date book. Do it today—don't wait. Throughout this book, I'll give you exercises to write in your Socializing Notebook and tell you how you are going to lay it out and use it over time. Ideally, you should do the exercises in the order in which they appear, but you don't want to rush them. The more thought you invest, the more revealing the results. Seeing things on paper versus just articulating them can make a big difference.

- Of course, as a writer, I tend to think of the benefits of the written word, but many of my clients have been surprised by their reaction after spending time on a given exercise. Before they began, their Socializing Notebook didn't strike them as something that would get them in better touch with themselves, but inner thoughts sometimes best show themselves on the page. So I hope you will give the exercises a shot!

Chapter 2 | ## *Act Like You Want to Marry a Mensch:*
WALK THE MENSCH WALK

You may ask, "Why all this talk about a mensch?" Perhaps you haven't heard the word before. You're going to have to trust me here in suggesting (or should I say demanding?) that you seek one out. Okay—do I sound too much like your mother, favorite aunt, or grandmother? The last thing I want to do is get on your back about it. However, let me say that you will absolutely *not* regret it if you are fortunate enough to find a mensch to share your life with. You will thank me afterward for impressing this upon you, and your mother will thank me, too. You don't have to invite me to the wedding, but I'd certainly love to hear from you if you find yourself living happily ever after with your MRM—Mr. Right Mensch.

The Mensch Factor

How do you know if someone has the "mensch factor"? And why should a mensch be the mate of choice? Because a mensch makes top-notch marriage material, assuming you are seriously looking to settle down. He represents all that is kind and true. In other words, he is emotionally healthy. The bottom line is, quite simply and emphatically put: Mensches rock! There is none better when you have marriage on the brain. Women in the know have for years sought out the mensch species because they are the very best in the "jungle" of dating. I hope you will do the same.

But before you can find your mensch, you must be able to identify a true one and be one to others and yourself. You need to walk the mensch walk . . . we'll call it the "mensch mile." You've heard the expression "until you've walked a mile in someone's shoes," meaning, until you've experienced what someone else has been through, you're not one to judge. In other words, be a master of your own "menschery," so you know how to find and marry one. Good attracts good—so work on your inner mensch. If you believe you deserve to find a good guy and invite the notion into your life, it's all the more likely to happen.

Mensch Myths Exploded

Let me dispel a few Mensch Myths that you might have on your mind. Take the following short quiz:

1. Does a mensch have to be Jewish?
2. Is a mensch the same as a schlep or a schlemiel?
3. Do mensches speak Yiddish?
4. Does circumcision make a mensch?
5. Can a Star Trek fan be a mensch?
6. Can a femme fatale be a mensch?

The answers are (1) no, (2) not at all, (3) some do, (4) no guarantee, (5) questionable (just kidding), and (6) absolutely.

How did you do? Do you need to brush up on the term?

MEASURE YOUR MENSCH FACTOR

How do you yourself measure up on the mensch scale? Do you have the mensch factor? Take the following quiz:

1. A close girlfriend calls. You just stepped out of the shower. She needs advice and wants you to come over, since her car broke down and she can't get to you. You:

   a. Tell her to eat some Ben & Jerry's ice cream and forget her sorrows.
   b. Suggest she call a car service and hightail it to your house.
   c. Give her the Web address for Dr. Ruth and suggest she drop her an e-mail.
   d. Throw a towel over your wet hair, put on some sweats, and zoom over to her place.

2. Your friend, on a serious budget, needs decorating advice, and she knows you're good at it. You:

   a. Say you'll help her and then send a bill for your time.
   b. Advise her up front that you can't do it for free.
   c. Tell her to watch a home-improvement show.
   d. Offer to go to Ikea together and help her pick out the perfect furniture.

3. You're doing your weekly food shop, and there's one already-cooked roast chicken left in the store. An elderly woman wants it, as do you. You:

   a. Take out a quarter and flip her for it.
   b. Willingly let her have it.
   c. Try to persuade her to buy the roast turkey breast instead.
   d. Stick it in your cart and run quickly to checkout, hoping she'll get over it.

4. Your neighbor desperately needs someone to watch her dog for a few days while she's away on an unexpected business trip. You've never had a pet before. You:

   a. Embrace the challenge and buy a book on proper dog care.
   b. Suggest she take the pooch to a kennel.
   c. Explain that you're honestly not comfortable watching the dog, since you have no prior experience.
   d. Tell her you hate dogs and she should get a bird.

5. You and your boyfriend dine out periodically with the same couple. Knowing they typically run up a much larger liquor tab than you, you:

   a. Decide in advance to split the tab, however it plays out.
   b. Grab the bill when it comes, whip out your calculator, and pay your calculated share.
   c. Order a three-pound lobster, hoping it will equal their liquor tab and even out the bill.
   d. Diplomatically suggest you get separate checks as couples.

6. You invite your parents over for dinner for the first time in your new apartment with your boyfriend. You cook a roast chicken, your signature dish, but are so nervous that you forget to clean the bird before you season it and put it into the oven. You:

   a. Explain and apologize to your parents, and order in Chinese food instead.
   b. Quickly send your mensch boyfriend to the supermarket to buy another chicken, and eat dinner later than planned.
   c. Serve the chicken anyway and hope no one notices.
   d. Cancel the dinner.

7. You are a week away from walking down the aisle with your betrothed mensch, and one of your bosses, whom you invited to the wedding, makes a comment that you're not working as hard these days, since you're getting married. You:

    a. Give him a written status report of all that you've done lately to prove he's wrong.

    b. Uninvite him to the wedding.

    c. Quickly change his table at the reception, so he's seated by the band's loudspeaker.

    d. Walk into his office and give him a piece of your mind.

8. Your boyfriend wants to go camping and asks you to go along, but you hate bugs and have never slept in a tent before. You:

    a. Suggest you take separate vacations.

    b. Buy some extra-strength bug spray and tell him you're game.

    c. Try to talk him into going to a spa instead.

    d. Tell him you'll go this once, but never again.

RESULTS:

A mensch would have answered as follows:

(1) d, (2) d, (3) b, (4) c, (5) d, (6) b, (7) a, (8) b

What *Is* a Mensch, Anyway?

I often get asked the definition of a mensch and how to know if someone fits the bill. My reply is that a real mensch will stand the test of time and be there for you through good and bad. You don't have to question his motives. We defined a mensch earlier as a decent, responsible person. More formally defined, a mensch is a person of integrity and honor, whether a man or a woman. In jest, I have heard the word menschette used to describe a woman, but there is no real basis for that. Other interpretations include a person having admirable characteristics, such as fortitude and firmness of purpose.

A mensch possesses the qualities one would hope for in a dear friend or trusted colleague—someone willing to give you the shirt off his or her back. A mensch shows respect for him- or herself and for others, and in return, commands respect. They are sensitive to the needs of others and want to help them. The term *mensch* comes from eastern Europe, and to refer to someone as such was considered the ultimate compliment. It takes true strength of character to earn the title of mensch, a way of being in the world that is reflected in all that he does. Imagine having the opportunity to walk down the aisle with one. How much better could a spouse possibly be as a person?

As we've established, mensches don't have to be Jewish. But if someone is Jewish and a mensch, does that make him all the more desirable? To some, the answer would be yes, because even some non-Jewish women (otherwise known as shiksas) crave the company of a mensch. They feel that Jewish men are the way to go, because they perceive them as being raised well and of good character. Many are stereotypically associated with big earnings potential, among other appealing traits. Shiksas on the make for mensches might go so far as to presume that all Jewish men are well-bred, wealthy, or mensches, but there are exceptions. Not everyone is a nice Jewish boy!

The "ersatz mensch" may try to pass himself off as one, but he is really a wolf in mensch clothing, so don't be taken in. Not all mensches are created equal. Decide for yourself what is most important in a mate, and look for those qualities when playing the mensch field. That way, you can identify the type of person who is best for you in the long run.

You deserve to be treated like gold, so don't ever sell yourself short, but do recognize that you can't get everything in one person. No one is perfect, so this is the time to curb your perfectionist tendencies if you have them. While it might be nice to have the "trophy husband," it's not all about looks, either, especially when it comes to mensches who potentially offer so much more.

While the term *mensch* literally means a "person" or "man," kindness and decency are not gender-specific, so, as stated earlier, a woman can be a mensch as well.

Real Mensches Don't Eat Just Matzo Balls: Chuck the Checklist and the Matzo Meal

A person need not be Jewish to be a mensch, as we've clarified. Mensches come in all sizes, shapes, sexes, and religions, and they don't necessarily love matzo balls or know how to make them. Each has his own menschisms, meaning manners, personality, and behavior. You must not judge people by how you think they should act based on preconceived notions or stereotypes. Establish what you want in a mate, but be open-minded. One more time: You can never get everything! This doesn't mean compromising standards, just being flexible and realistic and prioritizing.

Think about what makes for a good marriage. Look at couples you know who are happy. Do they talk to each other a lot? Are they both ambitious? Do they enjoy doing things together? Are they of equal intelligence? Do they both pitch in when it comes to taking care of the kids and/or their home? These are important questions.

A person is not bad just because he doesn't act as you would hope. You can't judge another's actions if they fall short of your own, unless you feel taken advantage of by them. If that's the case, the relationship isn't a healthy one. It is a lot to assume a love interest, or even a friend or family member, will meet all your expectations. One way to look at it is that all individuals dwell in their own world and have a belief system they create for themselves. Due in large part to our upbringing and past history, our belief system, which may well be false, will easily rule our thoughts and not allow us to respect the differences in people. It can also block you from meeting a mensch, because you are so fixated on making sure he "measures up" that no one will meet your sky-high standards.

We are influenced by what we perceive a marriage should be from witnessing our parents' marriage, good or bad. We were also each raised to believe that life has certain possibilities or limitations, and this influences our thinking. The right mate can potentially help you get past that, but ideally you are able to work on yourself so that you can make the best choice in a mensch and not look to someone else to make you whole or happy. You might be happier with a mensch by your side, but your MRM shouldn't be your sole source of joy. Often we choose mates to help us resolve issues from the past or even bring to the surface challenging relationships we've had with parents so we can learn to rise above them.

Take a look at a free spirit, if you know one. Free spirits live in the moment, don't overanalyze, go about their lives, etc. Notice how they may socialize with abandon and date up a storm. Perhaps because they live for today, they are able to take each date for what it's worth without attaching an outcome to it. Imagine how freeing that might be. Pretend you are a free spirit. Can you? Do you think it would empower you to date more? Would dates become more fun because you're less nervous about how each one might turn out? Would you open your mind to different types of people? Would your conversation be more upbeat because you're not focusing on your dating history, disappointments, etc.? Would you be able to stop trying to determine if each guy is Mr. Right Mensch (especially during the date) because you are placing greater reliance on your inner faith and trust that it will happen when it's meant to?

Give-and-take is part of any relationship, and we all come to a situation with a different set of values and experiences. These have an impact on our expectations of a mate. If you marry someone similar to yourself in terms of interests and attitude, it is more likely that you'll have a good marriage. One of the keys to a fulfilling relationship is knowing that you can actually live without one—that you'd be okay and could fend for yourself. It takes a lot of pressure off you if you aren't looking for someone to take care of you but, rather, someone to complement you.

LESSONS FROM THE LOVE COACH

When I was first married to my husband, I was amazed by how he went out of his way for people. It seemed that he put everyone before himself! Often his overtures of kindness and generosity were not returned to the same extent, but he didn't mind. If you share this trait and are okay with this, then it's fine, but you have to know yourself and not be disappointed and hurt when others don't deliver. And bear in mind that you don't want to fall in love with someone's "potential" and wait for him to come around to meet your standards. That day will almost certainly never come!

Act Like You Want to Meet a Mensch, Don't Just Think It

You need to make meeting Mr. Right Mensch a priority in your heart and mind. Many single people *say* they want to get married but don't *act* like they do. I mentioned this earlier but want to reinforce it here. These people think about it and are convinced that it's a priority, but when push comes to shove, they really aren't committed to making marriage a reality. If you take to heart just one message from this book, I hope it is this: Saying something and really wanting it enough to do something about it are two different things.

Does that make sense to you? Are you able to proclaim with complete conviction that you really want to get married sooner rather than later, or do you just think you do? You can save yourself a lot of agony if you admit that you can, in fact, live without becoming a Mrs. Mensch. There is nothing wrong with being single, but it's up to you to decide what you want for your future. Many people are unmarried, unattached, even celibate and happy. You have the choice.

Whose voice are you hearing in your head when it comes to marriage? Is it your own? Your mother's? Your father's? Your best friend's? The dry cleaner's? Your manicurist's? The postman's? The married mensch next door's? Is it society telling you that marriage is what you should want, rather than *you* saying it yourself?

Let's Get Started

It comes down to this: To find a mate, you must be open-minded, get out of the house, not judge someone in the first five minutes, and maintain a positive attitude. That may sound like a lot to think about, so let's start here. If you want to lose weight, it is often recommended that you use a visualization technique and act like a thin person. If you can imagine yourself slim, perhaps it will be easier to motivate yourself to spend more time in the gym, squeeze in that brisk walk around the block, and pass on the Milky Way or Ben & Jerry's Chunky Monkey ice cream that you routinely eat on a dateless evening when you're feeling sorry for yourself. Imagining can make it feel like something attainable. Sure, it's okay to indulge every now and then, but you don't want to make an ongoing date with Ben or Jerry!

Let's apply the same visualization principle to finding a mensch. Practice thinking like an active dater. Give people a chance. Have patience. Choose men who have the potential to take an interest in you. Schedule regular evenings out where you might meet someone. Get on the mailing or e-mail lists from organizations or social groups whose events interest you. Revamp your wardrobe if you think it needs an update. Try a new hair salon and change your look to see whom it attracts and if it makes you feel better about yourself.

> *To find a mate, you must be open-minded, get out of the house, not judge someone in the first five minutes, and maintain a positive attitude.*

When I once lectured about my first book, *How to Meet a Mensch in New York*, before a crowd of close to a hundred men and women in their twenties and thirties, I invited three of my single girlfriends to attend. It was a dinner social on a Friday evening after work. My presentation went over well, but as soon as it ended, I saw my friends in the rear of the room bolting for the door and sending me urgent hand signals to hurry so we could leave.

Before I could exit, however, I had to spend time signing copies of my book and giving personal advice to people approaching me with specific questions. As this happened, I was approached by three good-looking, seemingly nice, intelligent guys who wanted to chat with me. While I talked to them, my eyes quickly searched for my three girlfriends, who, of course, were nowhere to be found. All I could think of was what a lost opportunity for them to meet three potentially desirable men. It would have been worth a shot. Those guys certainly didn't come that evening solely to speak with me.

Afterward, driving home in the car, I asked my friends if they had fun and what they thought of the crowd. Not surprisingly, they labeled the evening "a big disappointment . . . a waste of time, and lousy food to boot." When I told them about the three guys I met, they said, "Oh, well. The crowd didn't look attractive overall, so we figured we would call it a night."

They lost out, and what a shame. While they made the effort to be there, were they really making a concerted effort to seize the socializing moment? What do you think? What would you say to yourself afterward if you were one of those women who missed an opportunity? Would you have even realized that perhaps you lost out? It would have been in their best interest to at least give it their all. Instead, they gave it a next-to-nothing try.

The lesson here is to take a hard look at your socializing efforts. It's not enough to put yourself in a place where you might meet someone if you have a habit of leaving a function or a party before you give people a chance, or typically spend time with the wrong kind of person for you. It takes some soul-searching and emotional strength to admit that there is more you could do to be a power socializer. You might have to seize the bull by the horns and make some major attitude adjustments, and that doesn't come easily for anyone.

WORDS OF WISDOM

Kelli Duckett, married ten months: "If a man is willing to give you the shirt off his back, he's always going to be there for you when you need him. If you have a problem, he will do everything in his power to make it better. That makes a mensch. If you are looking for a mensch, be open and willing to put yourself out there. You never know where or when he'll show up, so be ready. Working on yourself is helpful as well, so you can attract a healthy relationship."

Every Mensch Has a Mother

I can't end this chapter without addressing this critical topic. Every mensch has a mother, so what does that mean for you? True, you're not marrying his family, but he does come with a built-in set of in-laws, relatives, and perhaps siblings, and you will be the new kid in the *mishpocheh* if you stand at the chuppah (marriage canopy at a wedding).

When meeting your mensch's parents and other relatives, ask yourself this: Do they welcome you with open arms, or do you feel scrutinized? A little scrutiny is probably natural, but you don't want to feel like you're constantly being given the once-over. Do they express interest in your work and well-being? How do they get along with your parents and family? (At the very least, they have to respect and befriend one another at the wedding.)

Are these people you'd want to celebrate Thanksgiving with, among other holidays, birthdays, etc.? And what are their expectations of you once you join the family? Does his mother cook a family dinner every Friday night that you must religiously attend? Are you expected to buy a house on the same block they live on? And what if you have children? Will they be excited and supportive, or make you feel like you don't know how to be a good mother?

Working Things Out

A difficult in-law situation can create a lot of tension for you and your mensch, so it's important to know what you might be facing. I have heard many real-life stories on this subject, and it's amazing the challenges that in-laws can sometimes pose.

Risa, a friend, has discussed the pressure she feels because her in-laws live in Israel, and when they come to the States to visit several times a year, they expect to stay with her and her husband and their young child. While she and her husband have adequate space for his parents, Risa never knows exactly how long they'll be staying, and is expected to do their laundry, cook meals, etc., on top of taking care of her toddler son. And her husband does little to help, because he feels that this is a wife's "job." She loves her husband and accepts his belief system, but she has her moments of frustration and gets overwhelmed.

A woman I know, Kari, tells the story of her father-in-law and how he openly criticizes her in front of her young daughter as if she's an inadequate mother. She struggles to get him to respect her, but it's not easy.

Jill, a friend, has discussed with me how each time her mother-in-law comes to visit (thankfully for her sake, not often), she takes it upon herself to rearrange Jill's cabinets. She has a system for organizing dishes that she feels Jill should adopt. Jill is used to it, and has learned to try to look at it in a humorous way, but at the beginning, it felt demeaning.

This is not by any means to imply that it's not possible to have a warm, loving, inviting relationship with your future in-laws. It's also not to say that all family situations are perfect. If you are looking for that, finding a spouse will become that much more challenging. Have an awareness of the nature of the family you're potentially entering into, so you are not caught completely off guard. If your prospective in-laws are very different from you, that is okay, as long as there is mutual respect. You don't have to hang out together all the time, but you don't want to be at perpetual odds, either.

My friend Ellie and her husband bought a house right next door to his parents. They loved the area, and when the house unexpectedly came up for sale, they jumped on it. Ellie adores her in-laws, and even though they are next-door neighbors, they don't spend every waking moment together. However, being that close gives them all a strong sense of family and security, and that's a real bonus to any relationship.

Another woman I know, Tara, got married and bought a house in the same neighborhood as her parents but wound up living with her husband and her parents in her parents' house. Tara and her husband have been remodeling their house for several years now, but Tara admits that she is so close to her parents that they socialize as couples, and she doesn't know if they'll ever live in the house they bought. They might just wind up selling it and making a profit. Luckily, Tara's spouse is agreeable to living with her parents. But this cohabitation arrangement would surely not be for everyone!

The Mensch Doesn't Fall Far from the Tree

Remember that a mensch doesn't fall far from the family tree, so you want to take a look at his parents to get a better indication of who he really is. Do they appear to be mensches? Is their marriage solid and supportive? Are they excited that their son has found someone who makes him happy, or is his mother threatened by you? Of course, he won't be exactly like them, but you might get a sense of those qualities, good or bad, that he has inherited from his parents. It can help understand his attitude toward life if you spend some time talking with his folks and seeing how they view things. Were they raised during the Depression, and how did that affect them? Are they downbeat, critical people who rarely pay a compliment? What interests do they have? Is your future husband afraid to speak up to them?

If one or more of his parents are, sadly, deceased, then you obviously won't have the same opportunity. But you can also learn a lot about the kind of person your mensch is by noting his attitude toward a departed parent. How does he talk about his parents? Is it evident that he loved them? Does he discuss them often, and with fond remembrance? Does he display favorite photos of them? Does he walk around depressed over the loss even though it was quite some time ago? (This could be a red flag that he's never gotten over it.)

When you can marry a mensch and he comes with a mensch family, you have the best of all marital worlds.

EXERCISE:
Make Your Mensch Checklist

I hate the word *checklist*, but most people have one, so let's take a look at yours. Take out your Socializing Notebook. On a sheet, make two columns and list in one column fifteen qualities (if there are that many) that you are seeking in a mensch. In the other column, list what you don't want in a mate. Then cross out five traits from each column that you could accept not having on your list. What you have just created is a more realistic "checklist" of what to look for in someone.

Let me give you some idea of how to go about this: In the column with the traits you are seeking, you might look for such things as physical appeal, cleanliness, views toward life, desire for children, smarts, energy, chemistry, compassion, common sense, and relationship with family. In the column with those qualities you can't tolerate, give consideration to such things as dishonesty, unpleasant temperament, drug or alcohol usage, smoking, irresponsible spending habits, and gambling.

FROM PALS TO PASSION: GRACE AND ANGELO

Grace and Angelo met in high school drama class in their senior year. They became friends, and Angelo invited Grace to the prom. It was their first date (a pretty bold first date, I might add). After that, they went out for several months, and while they eventually broke up, they kept in touch occasionally over the years as friends.

When it came time for their ten-year high school reunion, both attended and felt an immediate attraction, but each was married or seriously involved at the time. Despite that, they developed a deep friendship and supported each other during difficult times in their lives, including both of them weathering a divorce.

Grace had met her first husband on a blind date and was married for five and a half years, and Angelo had met his first wife in school and was married for three years. Once the dust settled on their respective divorces, they decided to give a serious committed relationship a try, and wound up engaged nine months later. Six months after they were engaged, Grace and Angelo got married in St. Croix, U.S. Virgin Islands. Fourteen close family members and friends attended, and they later had a more traditional wedding reception with 125 guests. They now have been married for five years and have a toddler daughter.

MORAL OF THE STORY
A deep friendship can lead to a wonderful marriage, if you're open to it. Angelo proved himself a mensch, in particular when Grace's father was in the hospital and she eventually suffered his loss. Angelo's support and compassion were undeniable, and with their strong history of friendship, they had a powerful foundation for a marriage that would stand the test of time. So take a look at the friends you have in your life and see if there is romantic potential. You may be pleasantly surprised.

Chapter 3 | Clearing Out Your Baggage

In Chapter 4, I'll show you how to turn yourself into a "mensch magnet." But before you can learn what you *should* be doing, you need to take a good look at what you may be doing wrong—and fix it. I've found that the number-one mistake women make is getting too anxious about finding their very own Mr. Right Mensch. They project a "Help! I'm desperate!" attitude toward everyone they meet, including potential dates and mates. Before you can become a mensch magnet, you have to let go of the fears and worries that may be holding you back.

Learn to Play It Cool

Obsessing over love does not mean that you will find it any sooner than someone who is going about life in a happy, fulfilling manner. Try to calm down. Don't let it consume you. Most things happen when they are meant to, though we don't typically know why or when. You don't want to live just to get married—life is too short. Don't blame yourself for not being married. It isn't motivating to adopt a guilt-ridden attitude. You are where you are for a reason, and perhaps now you're ready to really do something to stir things up on the romantic front.

Love Your Life First: Lori's Story

I once did a love-coaching consultation with a woman named Lori who was in her late twenties and simply could not be happy until she became a Mrs. Mensch. A pretty blonde, she worked with children and yearned more than anything to be a wife, mother, and homemaker. She was trim, dressed to the nines, always wore makeup, painted her nails, and went to singles events like a woman on a mission.

Granted, persistence is not a bad thing; but Lori was going out far too often. Depression set in, and one day when I got a call from her, she was in a highly distraught state. She was crying hysterically because she had gone to a singles dance the night before, hadn't met anyone, and said she just couldn't take it anymore. That was her fifth dance in a week, and she was at the end of her rope. She felt like she was on a roller-coaster ride of socializing disappointment. Happiness was eluding her because she couldn't find anything good to say about her life. She felt like she would be eternally single and was petrified of that prospect. She was living almost exclusively for the love of one mensch.

Because I am not a therapist, I advised her to seek professional counsel, but it was sad to see such a young, appealing person with so much to offer in this heightened state of despair. We all have our moments, and you are certainly entitled, but you have to work to help them pass, so you can move on and achieve your greater marriage goal.

A little self-pity from time to time is okay and understandable. No one is immune from disappointment.

But if you're feeling self-pity or despair frequently, consider talking to a trained professional about it. You may even be able to find in your community a support group where people share their thoughts and challenges regarding dating. It might be comforting to you to hear what others have to say and know that you're not alone.

One of Lori's problems was that she had way too much time on her hands. Since she was a teacher, her typical workday ended by 3:00 p.m., and she was left with no plans for a good part of the day. One of my suggestions to her was that she consider doing volunteer work. Many singles I have coached complain that they have so little free time, and here was a woman who didn't know how to make the most of her after-hours availability!

I provided Lori with a list of appropriate nonprofit organizations, and she later told me that she had met a great guy through one of her volunteer efforts. But it didn't happen overnight! She was able to learn to curb her negative thoughts by focusing on the good she was doing for others. The act of volunteering took Lori out of herself, and that was exactly what she needed.

When we have too much time on our hands, it's an invitation for overanalysis of our lives. If you are open to changing things, that can be good; but if the voice inside you is highly critical, you're likely just to get down on yourself and feel all the worse. In Lori's case, meeting someone became icing on the cake, because it wasn't her focus when volunteering. In a perfect world, that would be the ideal way to meet someone. This plays into the notion of meeting someone when you least expect it because you're engaged in another activity, and Mr. Right Mensch happens to be there.

Living for the Love of One Mensch: Robin's Story

I know what it's like to live for the love of a desirable mensch. When I graduated from college and was working in New York City, I dated a guy named Ron for a few months. It didn't work out between us, because he had just finished graduate school and wanted to play the field, hang out with his friends, watch television in sports bars while he cheered for his alma mater's team, etc. I was crazy about him and thought he could be "the one," but we were on different wavelengths.

WORDS OF WISDOM

Janice Roberts, married thirty-three years: "There is absolutely no other kind of person to marry than a mensch. A mensch means friendship and respect. I would say that is the *only* one to marry! It's a guarantee that you will really enjoy a better life if you are with one. When you are trying to meet one, start off as friends first. See how supportive he is with your ideas, feelings, and thoughts. If he is not behind you 120 percent now, he never will be. The biggest problem in all relationships is that one person *thinks* the other will eventually change. They don't. *Once a mensch, always a mensch!*"

We ultimately broke up, and I ran into him with another woman at a party shortly thereafter. He hadn't wasted much time moving on, and I was shocked to see a new woman that quickly on his arm. I surmised that he must have been dating her while he was seeing me, and that made me feel rotten. It was bad enough that I wasn't with him anymore, but what made her more special than me? I reached all kinds of hurtful conclusions that basically added up to my feeling less than desirable. Yet he was with me for a while, so in reality, I couldn't be all bad. But that didn't matter. I wasn't able to think rationally about it.

My heart was so broken that at first I didn't know what to do with myself. After many a late-night crying session and relying on the patience and wisdom of close girlfriends, I decided what I needed most was to feel good about myself and to try to meet someone new. The part about wanting to feel good about myself was right on the mark, because I didn't want to let Ron bring me down. And my initial reaction had been that there must be something wrong with me because he dumped me. If you have ever had a breakup with someone, you probably understand where I was coming from.

I joined a gym, bought a bold new scarf and funky earrings, and decided I was going to make myself over—not in a huge way but just enough to lift my spirits and make Ron feel he was missing out on something terrific, if he were to run into me again. It was fun, and renewed my spirit (and wardrobe), but I was still the same person inside, and my heart needed time to heal. My head also had to clear so I could truly open my soul to someone new and connect in a meaningful way—not just feel like I was on the rebound.

Being on the rebound can be a quick route to misjudgment, if you don't catch yourself. You are more vulnerable and potentially inclined to pick someone for the wrong reasons because you need to reclaim your self-esteem. But really, self-esteem is an inside job, and another person can't be responsible for giving it to you. Even snagging a mensch isn't enough if you don't work on your own inner mensch.

WORDS OF WISDOM

Nicole Gould Levine, married nine years: "A mensch places you first, and that feels good. Because of my mensch's love, I am able to feel more grounded and self-assured. I know people will think that you shouldn't rely on someone else to make you feel special. I agree, but it still feels pretty darn great when you are on that pedestal! Mensches also take responsibility, and really want to understand the workings of a woman.

"If you want to marry a mensch, look for a sincere smile. Looks grow old—a good heart lasts forever. It's a good thing to be nurtured and loved by someone, so give the nice guy a chance. I hate the saying 'nice guys finish last.' It was probably mean, insecure people that started that phrase."

GETTING REALISTIC

If your "alone time" conjures up strong feelings of fear, then you might want to think about what you can do to strengthen your confidence. Perhaps you don't feel like you can take care of yourself? Or maybe you're insecure about truly functioning as an adult and living an independent life? For some, marrying a mensch can provide the ultimate sense of security. Most people would love that, but at the same time, you don't want to feel that you are truly dependent on someone else and that without him, you wouldn't make it in the world.

If you were blessed with supportive, loving parents while growing up, you have been raised with a strong feeling of being protected and adored. This is especially true if you consider yourself a "daddy's girl." How can anyone measure up to your image of the perfect man—your father? Where do you go from there? Even the utmost mensch has his own life to live! But it's true that while he may not be quite as selfless as your dad, he should make you feel loved and secure. That is a no-brainer. No doubt he will appreciate being needed, but you don't want him to feel that you are needy, because that implies weakness. So cut your potential mensch some slack, and let him be there for you in his own way without the dad comparison.

You want him to want you for the right reasons: because you are terrific, smart, engaging, fun to be around, etc. As much as you crave a mensch, you are okay on your own until the right one surfaces. If you say to yourself, "But I'm *not* all right . . .," you have hit the nail on the head in terms of what you might work on. You need to learn to take care of yourself, whether emotionally, physically, financially, or whatever. It's about being a whole person who can do more than just survive in the world—you could potentially take it by storm.

LOVE CAN OVERCOME A TABOO:
MELISSA AND AL

Melissa and Al have now been married eleven years. They met at work, where it was taboo to date a fellow employee. They had lunch several times a week and did a lot of things together as friends for a year. Melissa didn't know that Al was secretly in love with her. To hear her tell it:

"One day, he asked me if all the time we spent together meant as much to me as it did to him. He said he thought we could have a future together. I responded that I wasn't interested in dating him. He looked at his watch and figured he would stick it out for fifteen more minutes. Then I listed all of the reasons why it would never work. The more I listed, the more he figured he had a chance.

"The next few months were torture for Al. He basically agreed to do anything I asked him to do, because he was interested in me, and I was too thick to catch on. I used to say I could have asked him to play in traffic with me and he would have said yes. My girlfriends told me he liked me, but I didn't believe it.

"One night, we went out and had a horrible time. I gave him a peck on the cheek, which he thought was totally inconsistent with my saying I didn't want to date him. I still contend that I was acknowledging how he felt about me. I couldn't pretend that we were just friends when I knew he wanted more. He still says I was a messed-up chick. We joke that the worst date we ever had was with each other.

"On one of our dates, he came over to tell me he had had enough—that he didn't want to have anything to do with me anymore. But we wound up watching *West Side Story* on television, and he slowly put his arm around me. When the movie was over, he carried me into my bedroom, and the next day I got a dozen roses.

"By that time, he had left the company we both worked for when we first met, but he was now working for a competing company in the same industry. As a result, we were forced to keep our relationship a secret. When we got engaged, I had to go to five top executives at the company and tell them. I thought I would be fired, but they were surprisingly understanding. We wound up inviting our bosses to the wedding and seated them at the same table. These were people who normally avoided one another. We got a kick out of it, but must have changed the table arrangements twenty times before the wedding."

Melissa and Al are thrilled about their married life together and have a toddler daughter.

MORAL OF THE STORY

I'm sure you've heard the expression "Love conquers all." In this case, the fact that Melissa and Al worked for competing companies didn't stop them in their pursuit of love. So don't be afraid to forge ahead despite what might seem like an obstacle.

Additionally, in this particular case, Melissa is very fortunate that Al's love for her was strong enough for him to stick it out. The fact that someone may not seem like the type of person you think is good for you doesn't mean you shouldn't give him a try. Many women I spoke with for this book shared the fact that when they were single, they had a certain type in mind, but they actually wound up not marrying that type and were all the better for it.

In the end, if you marry a mensch, you won't have much to lose—but a huge amount to gain! Though, admittedly, you may not realize how lucky you are until you're in it and have the opportunity to look back on other choices you had made that were not as good for you.

Pacing Yourself: Robin's Story Continues

In my case, while I knew I was feeling needy and on the rebound, I couldn't help but yearn for someone new to fill the void in my heart. On top of it, since I've never been good about being laid-back when it comes to setting goals and striving to achieve, I pushed myself to socialize. It was another notch in my belt that I set my sights on. So, following my pattern, I established an aggressive socializing course for myself. And as if that weren't enough, I attached tremendous expectations to any effort I made to meet people.

[Give yourself credit for trying!]

Once I ventured back into the social scene, I was on the warpath. I went out as often as possible, with or without a friend. If no one was available, it didn't hold me back. I preferred not to go it alone, but didn't want that to stop my plan. I went to singles dances, tennis socials, fund-raising events, took classes—you name it. I felt like the Yellow Pages of dating, I was on so many mailing lists for singles groups.

When I went out, I'd initiate a conversation with a guy and try real hard to look approachable. Sometimes I'd get asked for my phone number, but more often than not, I wouldn't meet anyone who got me really excited. I was trying way too hard, and unbeknownst to me, it probably showed. I may not have had a deer-in-the-headlights look saying "Like me . . . date me," but giving off vibes isn't necessarily obvious in that way. Looking back, I'm sure I gave off major vibes of anxiousness, and that's not appealing. In my highly emotional state, I was oblivious to how I might be coming across.

My lack of socializing success further depressed me because I yearned for Ron. What I eventually realized was that I was putting too much pressure on myself to get back out there and replace him. I compared everyone I met with him, and in my eyes at the time, no one could measure up. What did I want from myself? And what was I expecting in someone else? I was clearly looking for the impossible: a Ron clone ready for commitment. How unrealistic was that?!

Once I came to terms with my mind-set, I learned to pace myself and scale back my number of nights on the town. I still went out, but tried not to attach an outcome to each of my efforts. I patted myself on the back for whatever effort I did make. It's important to do that—to allow yourself to feel good about your endeavors. Give yourself credit for trying.

I also gave myself the benefit of the doubt in terms of trusting my gut that somehow one day my mensch would come along. And he would want me as much as I wanted him. I deserved that, and you do, too. One day you'll look back, when you're old and gray and sitting in a rocker next to your Mr. Right Mensch, and you'll wonder what you ever worried about.

Accept the Chuppah Challenge

So you want to make it to the chuppah. It is not impossible to get a walk down the aisle, even if it seems like an unattainable feat. In actuality, if you think about it, anyone can tie the knot. The state of matrimony itself, however, is no great accomplishment. It is not a panacea. The real challenge is to be married and happy and make it work over the long run.

Before you attempt to meet Mr. Right Mensch, you must take a look at yourself and be reasonably content with who you are and what you've done thus far with your life (even if it hasn't turned out exactly as you had planned). You may have heard the saying "We make our plans, and God makes His." That couldn't be truer. While we can't control our destiny, we can control our attitude and our reaction to what happens to us.

[*You need to achieve personal contentment before you can find love.*]

If you're not happy with yourself, you can't expect someone else to make you happy or even want to be with you. A content single person can be a merrier married person, assuming you choose the right mate. And you can really be confident of choosing the right mate—a mensch—only when you're in a good place in your own life. Then you know you'll be making decisions with a clarity that will help you avoid making a mistake that might lead to divorce.

People get married for all kinds of reasons, and you want to walk down the aisle, elope in Aruba, or tie the knot in the Las Vegas Chapel of Love for all the right reasons. You will know in your heart when that is the case, and if you're not sure, that's your answer right there. A love-coaching client of mine who is divorced and considering settling down once again with her new boyfriend asked me the question "If you've met a good catch, how do you know if you're settling or if you are really in love?" The short response is: If you have to ask the question, you know the answer. To expand on that, marriage can become routine or predictable after a while, but if you've chosen the right person, you'll want to keep it interesting because you know this is the person you are committed to, not just out of legal obligation but because your decision is heart-driven.

It is tempting to want to be with someone, especially if money is an issue for you and he is very financially secure and generous. Having money can definitely make life easier, but it doesn't guarantee happiness. If you are forty plus, you may feel you have fewer opportunities for marriage, but really, you can meet your *beshert* at any age. People do find true love later in life. If you don't believe it, read the Sunday *New York Times* one weekend and check out the wedding announcements. I love to do that, because it's great to see couples of all ages and backgrounds exchange vows, whether for the first or the third time. While I don't know them personally, I have to believe that for some (hopefully, for most), they are tying the knot with a true love—and, ideally, a mensch.

Marriage is a big step, and one that might feel overwhelming because it's a huge change in your life. If you're getting cold feet, it's essential that you ponder this question: Is it the notion of marriage that scares you or is it marriage to this person? If you have any doubt and learn to trust your instincts, you will be able to assess which is the case and move forward with conviction. Remember, when you get married, "It's about being yourself, only with someone else," as the mother of Anne Hathaway's character says in the film *The Princess Diaries 2*.

LESSONS FROM THE LOVE COACH

Sometimes we need to assess the people in our lives to determine if they make us feel good about ourselves. You want to surround yourself with as many positive, supportive people as possible, especially if you're going through a rough period or a life change. I have always believed in the power of good friends to help spur us on to reach our goals, even when we have moments of giving up on ourselves.

EXERCISE:
Would You Date Yourself?

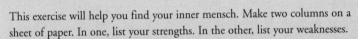

This exercise will help you find your inner mensch. Make two columns on a sheet of paper. In one, list your strengths. In the other, list your weaknesses.

Think about which of your strengths would be most appealing to the opposite sex, and place a star by those listings. Now think about what weaknesses you might work on so you feel that you're really putting your best self forward. Underline those items, and on a separate page, list them with spaces between them. Then give it some thought, and try to identify what steps you might take toward overcoming each weakness, if it is something that can be changed.

Another way to look at a weakness is to view it as an insecurity. It's not necessarily a bad trait, but perhaps it's something that isn't serving you or something that you've long thought you could improve upon. If you're not certain, you might even enlist the help of a close friend. Sometimes it's hard to see ourselves, and a third party can be immensely helpful and lead to greater clarity so you can zero in on your inner mensch.

The One-Sided Date—and How to Avoid It

Have you gone on a date and thought everything went smashingly, only to find out after the fact that the guy has no intention of calling again? It was good only for *you*. (And I'm *not* talking about sex!) How is that possible? Did the conversation lag? Was there no attraction? A lack of chemistry, perhaps?

Unfortunately, it is possible to have a one-sided date. But how can you know if it's happened to you? While it is hard to be certain at the time, and you don't want to dissect the situation during the date, with practice, you can learn to get a good read on the vibe of the date.

The Brainy Bore: Dennis's Story

One of my love-coaching clients, Dennis, forty-four, was a notorious "one-date Charlie," so to speak. He rarely got past the first—or the rare second—date with the women he took out. Before meeting his wife (thanks to an introduction), he went through dates like water. The problem was that he was clueless when it came to knowing how to please a woman.

Dennis was definitely a mensch, so there were no ill intentions, but he often didn't have a comfort level. Because of that, he'd wind up talking predominantly about work, which in his case was quite technical, since he was an engineer. The woman, for the most part, didn't understand much of what he was discussing. And while she'd act interested to be polite, it was the kiss of death. Most didn't want a second date with him, or if they gave him another try, that was the last of it.

As nice as Dennis was, the dullness of the dates could not be overcome. To the women he dated, it felt like very self-centered conversation—a monologue rather than a dialogue. He was actually a bighearted guy, but it was hard for women to perceive that when he talked endlessly about (as they perceived it) himself and didn't really include them much.

Dennis, not picking up on the vibes of his dates, was often surprised when he'd call the women for another date. He thought they had clicked, since the date was fun for him. Fortunately for Dennis, I was able to assess his situation and give him "remedial training" to help him connect with others, so women could see beyond the outer engineer to the inner mensch.

Making Sure a Date Is Two-Sided

The takeaway from Dennis's story is that making small talk doesn't come naturally to all people. It doesn't mean that they're not mensches, but perhaps they need time or training to be able to present their best self. Be sensitive to the fact that it takes two to click.

As I mentioned earlier, listening is an important skill to have, and one of the reasons a date might come across as one-sided is that the other person doesn't feel like you're really "with" him. Perhaps your thoughts are elsewhere because you're preoccupied with your To Do list, or you have such a crush on this person that you feel like you're walking on eggshells.

You don't want to mess up the date or the relationship potential, but keep in mind, the other person doesn't know that. He may interpret your actions as lack of interest and, fearing rejection, might not pick up the phone to ask for a second date. Give him your full attention, act like you're enjoying yourself (and him!), remember to participate but not dominate the conversation, and you'll have a much better chance of getting to that next date.

Aliza Sherman Risdahl, married one and a half years: "There is too much competition, divisiveness, negativity, and outright meanness in the world. To be able to make a life and a home with a positive and loving person, a mensch, is a blessing.

"If you want to marry a mensch, you first have to believe you deserve a mensch. If you suffer from low self-esteem, chances are you will pick a person who treats you in a way you believe you should be treated: badly. If you love yourself and like yourself, you will most likely choose the right man for you, someone who will treat you how you deserve to be treated: like a precious and rare individual, like a good person.

"I remember that when my husband and I were dating, and I finally realized how good he was for me, I told him that I deserved him. He thought that was such an odd choice of words—that someone could deserve someone else. Now he gets it, and he thinks he deserves me, too. We all deserve someone who will be good to us, love us, and make us feel good about ourselves."

A SENSE OF HUMOR GOES A LONG WAY: LISA AND PAUL

Lisa took out a personal ad in *New York* magazine when she turned thirty. She was feeling good about herself, having just returned from a fun and relaxing trip to Club Med in Mexico. She had gone with a close friend from college, and both of them were single. Lisa was looking to meet someone to enjoy the summer with—the beach, concerts, picnics, long walks on New York City streets after work, etc. Hesitant to get her hopes up, she wrote the ad in a light frame of mind. She wanted to meet someone who would share her sense of humor and appreciate laughter and silliness.

Her ad began as follows: "If you're into naked bungee jumping. . ." She received replies from sixty men, including one who was in jail. After three weeks, she went on a date with Paul, the man who was to become her husband. Paul liked her ad because he thought it was funny and clever. The day of their date, it was 105 degrees, and Lisa remembers it well. She and Paul had drinks and hit it off, with lots of laughter and fun chatter, smiles, and even some hand-holding.

Their second date was less than a week later, and three months later they became engaged. Four months after that they were married. After eleven years of marriage, they now have a dog and a toddler son, and still give each other two anniversary cards each month, on the date they met and the date of their wedding. Their relationship is built on romance, and they make sure to incorporate it into their lives on an ongoing basis.

To hear Lisa tell it, "Paul is a definite mensch, because he is a good, caring, loving husband who treats me like gold and would do anything for those he is close to, me and others included. He is a great father, loving and devoted, and a gentleman, always."

MORAL OF THE STORY

Lisa wasn't afraid to have fun with her ad. She was clear that laughter plays an important role in her life and didn't hesitate to write the ad with levity. She was serious about wanting to meet someone but didn't get hung up when it came to choosing her words. So . . . just go for it. Don't overthink when you are writing an ad. Having a sense of humor is a great way to break through the clutter and get your ad noticed.

Chapter 4 | *How to Be a Mensch Magnet*

In Chapter 3 we looked at how you can sabotage yourself on your way to becoming a mensch magnet. Now I hope you've taken a good, hard look to see just how many of these mistakes and stories might well apply to you, and have resolved to do something about it. So let's start making those changes by talking a bit about magnetism.

Upping Your Mensch Magnet-tude

Do you have a magnetic personality? Do people just naturally gravitate to you? If so, you are one step ahead in the socializing game. If not, do you know someone like that? The life of the party? Is there a friend you socialize with who often gets approached by men? If you wish this would happen to you, but you're tired of waiting for it, you have the power to take matters into your own hands and become a mensch magnet. So, here's Mensch Magnet Rule #1: Make your own move!

You can become someone people want to get to know, even if it doesn't come naturally. Somebody's got to make eye contact, so why not you? No reason to wait for the man to approach you. It's the early bird that catches the worm, and I would rather play the role of the bird, not the worm. Wouldn't you?

Consider this scenario: You're at a singles event or party, and you've nursed three ginger ales in two hours trying to occupy yourself while waiting to be approached by a desirable man. I am a firm believer that if you wait for him to initiate, you may be old and gray—and still solo—before you even realize it. Take matters into your own hands. There's a big difference between being assertive and being aggressive. I'm not talking about declaring your love. I'm simply suggesting that you might jump-start a conversation.

[Mensch Magnet
Rule No. 1:
Make your own move!]

I'm also not suggesting that you propose a date. However, if you don't risk rejection, it might take you longer than necessary to find true love. The only person who never gets rejected is the one who doesn't try. Playing it safe is a waste in this instance. Why limit yourself to people who approach you? The average guy will likely welcome your reaching out, and if he doesn't, he's not for you, so who cares? Maybe you remind him of his mother or his ex. If he rejects you, he doesn't know you, so you really have no reason to take it personally. It's his loss. You'll bounce back.

If he *does* respond to your introductory overture, remember, it doesn't mean you're easy to get in the long run, so don't get hung up thinking about "rules." Could be he's shy and needs a little encouragement. Maybe he has had a rough day and can't motivate himself to flirt—or maybe he doesn't know how! Whatever the reason, you'd be doing a mitzvah (good thing) if you helped the potential mensch out. I will discuss props and flirting beginning on page 71, and will offer specific tips on how to best approach someone or catch his eye.

LOOKING GOOD, FEELING GREAT

Feeling good about yourself includes feeling good about your appearance. If you wish you could lose weight and want to be proactive about it, get moving. Buy a treadmill or go for regular walks with a friend. Get a pedometer and count your daily steps. Experiment with Pilates or yoga.

If you want to update your wardrobe and don't know where to start, consider consulting a personal shopper at a department store or seek out an image consultant. They are there to make suggestions and help you make flattering fashion choices.

If you are itching for a new hairstyle or approach to makeup, flip through magazines and cut out pictures so you can show them to a new hair stylist who might have fresh ideas. Some specialized salons even have computers that can churn out different images of you with varying hairstyles, so you can see in advance how they may look. A new hairstyle or color can make such a difference. It can perk up your whole attitude!

Many department store makeup counters periodically feature trained makeup artists who are there for the day doing makeovers. You might consider going this route to get ideas and have fun. Grab a girlfriend and make it an afternoon out. First impressions are important, and you want to put your best foot—and face!—forward so you can project the confidence it takes to attract the mensch you want by your side.

MENSCHES ARE FROM MARS (OR IT SOMETIMES SEEMS THAT WAY!)

Sometimes we want the answer as to why guys—even mensches—behave as they do. I've come to accept that it's not that simple. I do believe that men don't do anything they don't want to do, but if you were to ask them to explain their motivation, they might not be able to articulate it. They are much more black and white than women are. Something either works for them or it doesn't, and it might not seem rational to us.

Of course, all of us have our own style of dating. We approach it based on our own history, concerns, fears, upbringing, expectations, etc. Most of us are looking for true love and companionship and have the best of intentions. But we sometimes have a funny or unpredictable way of showing it, so our potential love interest may get thrown off. It has to do with the world we create for ourselves and how we live in it.

Since we all perceive relationships differently, it's very exciting when we click with someone, especially if there is chemistry from the beginning. But if someone is truly hard to understand or exhibits inconsistent behavior, do yourself a favor and don't spend endless time and grief overanalyzing. Depending on the circumstances, you might be well served not to stick around too long—at least unless you can prove that the relationship is important to him and there is commitment potential.

Mensch Magnet Rule No. 2:
A social setting is not
a battleground, so don't surround
yourself with troops!

A SOCIAL SETTING IS NOT A BATTLEGROUND

Here's a tip to keep in mind if you usually find yourself socializing with a group of female friends. If you attend a party or other social gathering, it's great to go with cohorts, but you don't want to surround yourself with other women as though you were glued together at the hip (especially if it's Krazy Glue!). You must split up; otherwise, it may be intimidating for someone to approach you and break through the "troops." Have a plan to circulate solo and meet back at a certain spot within a designated time period. Give yourself ample time to get around without feeling pressured.

Always Have a Prop

If you want to encourage people to approach you, have a prop. What do I mean? Something conversational that might catch someone's eye. (I'll talk more about this on page 72.) A prop gives a person something to talk about—and an excuse to approach you—if he wants to initiate a conversation with you. For example, a good prop might be as simple as a T-shirt with a catchy phrase or logo that reflects an interest you have, or perhaps a funny saying, your favorite vacation spot or sports team. You might strike a chord with someone who likes the same resort as you or roots for the same team.

Going to the Dogs

Dogs are among the best people magnets, so they make perfect props. When I was single and working in New York City, out of curiosity, I spent one evening at a dog run. This particular one was on the Upper West Side and had a reputation as a hot spot for single dog lovers. While I didn't have a dog, I decided to visit anyway after work to check out the scene. And what a scene it was! There were about a dozen or so dog owners, both men and women, mingling while their pooches ran wild in a fenced area. I had never witnessed anything quite like it. Had I known what to expect, I would have thrown on overalls or sweats, but at least I had a chance to talk to new people. What was intriguing was that people knew one another through their dogs. They even knew the other dogs' names!

You don't have to frequent a dog run to benefit from the presence of a dog. If you don't have one, borrow one, and take it for a walk on a busy street. If it is a cute or eye-catching canine, you'll be surprised how many people may stop you on the street or make comments, and before you know it, a conversation is flowing. I once met a woman who put a cat on a leash and took it for a walk. I'm not advocating that you put just any animal on a leash and parade it around town, but dogs can be terrific icebreakers.

Mensch Magnet Rule No. 3: Make yourself more magnetic by always wearing or taking along a good prop.

Give Yourself an Edge

Besides a cute dog, examples of props include articles of clothing or accessories. Consider the following: You work out at a gym three times a week, or jog in your neighborhood, or go rock climbing on the weekend. Instead of your usual sweatshirt, what about wearing a T-shirt with a striking saying or design? It could be something funny, or from your alma mater, or your favorite rock group or Broadway show. There are so many choices, and they offer the perfect conversation opener. Go online and see what you can turn up on the Web, or, if you live in a big city like New York, check out a museum gift shop or fashion-forward places like Greenwich Village or SoHo, where shops sell all kinds of cool T-shirts, baseball caps, etc.

If you're going someplace more formal, another type of prop would be an interesting pin or hat, or a colorful belt or scarf. Again, it's an item that someone may notice and approach you to comment on. In turn, you may do the same if you see someone wearing something that grabs you. If you don't want to spend a lot on it or want something really original, check out your local flea market or craft fair, or even go on www.eBay.com. You'd be surprised what you can find.

It's all about standing out in a crowd and giving yourself an edge. You want to make it easier for someone to chat with you by giving him a more natural entrée. It's not easy for most people to make conversation, but you are inviting them in, so to speak, by attracting them in the first place and presenting a conversation opener.

Be an Opportunist and Flirt

You never know when a prime opportunity will present itself, so seize the moment. If you see someone who looks interesting, make a move. Test your mensch magnet mettle! Opportunities to meet an appealing person are sometimes fleeting, and if you don't go for it, you'll be left with only regret.

I was once on vacation at a resort during a singles weekend and had an accident while on the tennis court. I was playing doubles and got hit squarely on the bridge of my nose with my partner's oversized tennis racket. While it was a very painful and embarrassing experience, I met nearly every eligible doctor at the hotel, as they were quickly summoned to my court to administer first aid. Had I been a good flirt at the time, I might have had a real opportunity to take advantage of the situation. But I was a bit on the shy side and was understandably preoccupied with my injury (and not looking my best!).

FROM *TSURIS* (DIFFICULTY) TO *SIMCHA* (JOYOUS OCCASION): MIKKI AND ALAN

Mikki and Alan met for the first time when they were thirteen and fourteen, respectively. Alan was the best friend of Mikki's brother, and they are best friends to this day. Mikki had just had a major back operation and was immobile in a body cast, in her pajamas, lying in a hospital bed in her family's apartment. Alan came to visit her brother, and to Mikki's embarrassment, that was how they were introduced.

After that initial meeting, they saw each other from time to time at such events as her brother's high school graduation and wedding, though they didn't have any kind of conversation. She never for a moment thought of Alan romantically, mostly because he shared many similar traits with her brother, who was the complete opposite of Mikki. Both guys loved The Grateful Dead, had long hair, partied a lot, weren't into school, etc.

Mikki had several relationships during college and law school and dated quite a bit before she went out with Alan. In college and law school, she seriously dated two other mensches (though neither one worked out, mostly due to timing), but since then, no mensches came into her life until Alan.

When Mikki was forty-one, she held a memorial service in New York for her beloved grandmother, who had passed away at one hundred years of age. Alan, forty-two, and another friend of her brother's, attended the service. Mikki's own brother had been unable to make it, yet Alan was there, standing in for him, in a sense, according to Mikki. Mikki was very touched by his taking the time to be there, especially since he was now living in Colorado and was in town only to attend various family functions. Alan hugged her when he said goodbye and said that he considered Mikki and her brother family, and that she should let him know if there were anything he could do.

That night, two of Mikki's close girlfriends stayed over so she wouldn't be alone. Each asked, "What about Alan?" since they knew she was single and looking. Mikki, however, dismissed their question, since she had never thought about Alan that way.

Early the next morning, the phone rang, and it was Alan. He said he was going to be in town another week and would like to have dinner. Even though she was shocked that he called, and even more that he asked her out, she thought it was just a friendly invitation from her brother's best friend who was trying to be nice and take her mind off the loss of her grandmother. They had drinks at a chic spot in New York, followed by dinner at a quaint café, and they talked nonstop for five hours.

Before the date ended, Alan said that he was uncertain about pursuing a long-distance relationship, since he had never done so before, but knew that he wanted to see her again. Mikki knew that she didn't want to say good night and thought they potentially had some sort of future together, though she didn't dare dream that this could be her "forever." She was cautious due to past experience. However, once they had their next date, Mikki allowed herself to feel all of those emotions and to let her heart go there.

They dated nine months before getting engaged, with each flying back and forth (Mikki lived in Connecticut), and e-mailed and/or talked every day. They married eight months after Alan proposed, and Mikki's brother was the best man. Mikki had lost her dad when she was thirty (her dad was fifty-nine), so it was very special to have her brother by her side, for more reasons than one.

Mikki often thinks that it was her grandmother who brought Alan into her life. They had been very close, and since she was no longer there, Mikki believed it was her grandmother's doing that she find Alan and marry for eternity. Additionally, Mikki admitted that she was then truly ready for someone like Alan and what he represented. During her dating years, nineteen to thirty-five or so, she had been fearful of such a huge commitment. Her mom had been married three times, leaving Mikki to question whether she could do a good job as a wife and keep up her end of a relationship.

She didn't want to wind up like her mother, and wondered if it was her destiny. So the easy thing to do was to avoid it. Then, on top of it, when she lost her mother at the age of twenty-four (her mom was just forty-six), it left her feeling so empty that she didn't want to get married and then divorced, as the pain would have been "insufferable," in her eyes.

When Mikki reached thirty-five and felt ready to get married and have a family, she feared that the worst fate in life would be to "wake up one morning and look across your bed, and be married to a man with whom you were not in love." That thought sometimes led her to date the wrong man for too long, as she thought maybe her mind would change and he'd grow on her. Ultimately, she made the right choice with Alan, and they now happily live in Colorado, and have an infant daughter.

MORAL OF THE STORY

You can't let fear rule your life. And if we're open to it, love may be found in unexpected places, at any age. Timing is so important, as we discussed earlier. You can meet the same person at different times in your life, and if it's meant to work out, it will when the universe supports the notion. There is no way to predict, but if you believe, as I do, that everything happens for a reason, you can have faith in knowing that if you want something badly enough, it can happen for you. Sometimes it's right under your nose and you don't even realize it. From bad can come good—like the passing of Mikki's grandmother, which led to Mikki and Alan's finding each other later in life. So hang in there, despite any discouragement.

Additionally, it's important to realize that we don't have to follow in our parents' footsteps. If your parents had or have a good marriage and serve as positive role models, you are very fortunate. Not everyone has that. But we can shape our own destiny. Part of it is believing that you deserve good and can actually help manifest it. We aren't responsible for our parents' challenges, nor is it written in stone that we will face the same fate.

> Mensch Magnet
> Rule No. 4: Be an
> opportunist and flirt!

The Fine Art of Flirting

Flirting is the playful art of catching someone's eye. It can be done with a simple smile and show of receptiveness through open, positive body language. If you aspire to be a mensch magnet, review the following lists of dos and don'ts for flirting…and practice. These tips can help you attract a mensch or have the confidence to approach one.

FLIRTING DOS:

- *Be a good listener*—silence can be sexy. It's not a contest to see who talks the most or fastest, unless you're my friend Fran, the official World's Fastest-Talking Female. When you engage in discussion with someone, gaps in a conversation are natural. Don't try to constantly fill them. Give the other person a chance to jump in. Don't get nervous if the conversation does not flow right away. Some people take time to warm up to someone new. Additionally, if you can be a good listener, that is so appreciated. All of us like to feel that someone is genuinely focused on us and is taking in our every word with thoughtfulness.

- *Don't forget your prop.* I often get asked about flirting tricks of the trade. One of the best tips I can offer is to have a prop—or respond to one!—when you're trying to connect with someone. I mentioned the importance of props on page

71, but it bears repeating. A prop could be anything that catches someone's eye and invites (ideally positive) comment.

- *Make direct eye contact.* The key to flirting is to make sure you connect with the other person. If you are on the shy side, it's easy to think that you have caught someone's eye, when, in fact, he is oblivious to your overtures. You want to look someone straight in the eye, look away, and look back, so that you've connected more than once and you've made it clear that you are looking at him. Don't stare…just catch his glance in a friendly manner.

- *Smile and exhibit positive, open body language.* Once you have made direct eye contact with someone, you want to smile and look like you're receptive to meeting him. This is done by maintaining open body language. For example, you don't want to stand with your arms crossed. If it helps you to hold something, buy a drink or grab a glass of water and keep it in one hand. If your arms are crossed, you're closing yourself in and may look stiff. When you are talking to someone, lean in toward him. It shows that you are not afraid to get close to him—though not *too* close, unless you're looking for a fling and want to get touchy-feely.

- *Pay a compliment, make someone laugh, or ask a question.* Besides commenting on someone's prop, other approaches are to pay a compliment, make someone laugh, or ask a question when initiating a conversation. If you're paying a compliment, you want to keep it "clean." The goal isn't to embarrass someone but to make him feel good about himself. To make someone laugh, again, you don't want to be offensive, and humor can be very subjective. No dirty-joke telling until you know if it's his style! Don't be afraid to giggle and show that you are entertained, if

Mary Ellen Friedmann, married nine and a half years: "A mensch is someone who has a kind heart and treats your needs as his own. Life is too short to waste time playing games. If you feel genuinely comfortable and loved with this person, that's how your children (if you want a family) are going to feel growing up. It's important to your sense of well-being to find someone who reflects you and the goodness in you. We all have bad days and not so happy moments, but overall, a mensch should elevate you and match the best of you. It is a choice you make.

"If you are looking for a mensch, my advice is to see the man for who he is, how well people respond to him, and how he treats others. My husband never had an enemy. He never trashed ex-girlfriends to me. Every ex-boss, old friends, and others have had only nice things to say about him, and that means a lot."

the joke strikes your funny bone. Most men love the fact that you're not afraid to laugh. It can be a turn-on.

Asking a question is the most neutral and natural way to go, as long as you don't get overly personal right away. For example, if you're at a neighborhood happy hour at a restaurant you frequent, you can approach someone by asking if he lives nearby and what his favorite local restaurants are. If you're in a gym, you can ask a guy how to use a particular weight machine, as long as you don't pester him too much during his own workout. It is flattering to be asked to share your knowledge, and this can be the equivalent of paying a compliment, because the other person will feel that you consider him worthy of offering instruction.

FLIRTING DON'TS:

- *Don't get too touchy.* There's a fine line between flirting and sexual harassment. You don't want to get overly touchy with a stranger or invade someone's personal space. When approaching someone, stay a comfortable distance from his face and don't touch his body in an inappropriate manner. It can offend a person or, at the very least, turn him off.

- *Know when the answer is no.* Along with not getting too touchy comes the need to understand when to take no for an answer. It's important to hear someone loud and clear and not dismiss his response if he isn't reacting positively. Don't take it personally. He doesn't know you, so who knows what his reasoning is?

- *Don't overanalyze when trying to approach someone.* If you overthink a situation, before you know it, the opportunity to act may be lost. There really is no perfect way to flirt. The worst thing would be not to try because you're scared or trying to come up with the ideal approach. You'll kick yourself afterward if you don't just do it.

- *Don't force yourself to go out if you're in a bad mood* (unless you're always in a bad mood). While you might feel like you need to go out as much as possible to try to meet someone, there's honestly no point if you're not mentally up to it. Now, you might say, "I'm never really up to it." And I would understand, because it's not always easy putting yourself out there, especially after a hard day at the office. Transitioning from work to play doesn't come naturally to everyone. If you're burned out and really want to go home and chill, do it. Just don't give in to yourself constantly, because you may *never* go out!

- *Don't be afraid to laugh!* It's attractive . . . and contagious. If you're out with friends, don't be afraid to show that you're having a good time. If you come across as a fun-loving person, that will suggest that you're someone who likes to enjoy herself, appreciates friends, and welcomes the opportunity for a good laugh. You know how to let your hair down, and sharing that zest for life is something you'd love to do with the right person. Who wouldn't want to meet you if he picks up your perky personality?

- *Don't look around for other prospects when you're talking to someone.* The kiss of death for a potential love interest is for him to catch your eye wandering while the two of you are talking. You've flirted your heart out and connected with someone—now don't blow it by overtly checking out others around the room. If you think he won't notice your distraction, you're wrong. (*You* notice when someone's doing it to you, don't you?) This has to do with living in the moment, as well. Take time to talk to the person in front of you, as opposed to wondering who else is there. You might miss out on a great person if you are busy scoping out the room . . . and the grass isn't always greener.

- *Don't start searching for a pen or a piece of paper if you meet someone.* One of the best ways to lose an opportunity to get someone's number or give out yours is to be ill prepared. Always have a business or personal calling card available. (If you don't want to pay a lot for one or aren't sure where to start to make one up, check out www.vistaprint.com.) If you're scrounging around for paper, a pen, or even a napkin to write on, it can become embarrassing and kill the potentially romantic moment. Plus, you may prefer to be subtle in a crowd when you give out your number, and having a card is the most discreet way to pass on your information. If you're not certain you want to give out your home number, consider your cell number.

PRE-DATE COMMUNICATIONS

I've already recommended business or calling cards as a way to give a prospective date your name and number. Additionally, you might want to create an e-mail account for socializing purposes, so that you can also give out that e-mail address. I caution you, however, not to get too personal if you e-mail each other. It's easy to get caught up in the exchange and even forget that you are writing to a real person. Use e-mail just as a means to arrange a date. Don't rely on it initially as a big information-sharing vehicle. It is way premature to take that approach.

I have seen people practically fall in love before the first date because they felt such a strong e-mail connection. The same holds true for the phone. Try not to talk for hours on end before you've had a date. You might think this is indicative of a heartfelt connection, but that's not necessarily true. It takes time to be certain of that, and in the interim, it can be more hurtful to grow attached to someone before you've spent quality time in person and can see if the connection is there beyond the phone and the Internet.

Denise McDonald, married two and a half years: "I believe lasting relationships are based on a foundation of trust, and a mensch epitomizes that. If you have an untrustworthy, unreliable partner who always makes you second-guess his honesty and whereabouts, you'll never be able to relax and enjoy life with this person. Unfortunately, some women get a high from that constant uncertainty—living on that ledge. If you want to meet a mensch, try to meet him through a mutual acquaintance or through your church or synagogue. Work is also a great place to assess someone's personality under stress. Be sure that you know others who know him and can help you gauge his 'menschworthiness.'

"During my search for a mensch, I found three things very telling: how he acted in a competitive situation, such as a game of golf or cards; how he treated the waitstaff at a restaurant; and how he behaved on a road trip. If he had a hot temper on the golf course or during a friendly game of cards, that was a red flag. If he treated the waitstaff rudely and dismissively, rather than with patience and kindness, he was no mensch. If he could drive a car without road rage, be patient when I had to stop often for bathroom breaks, and still be pleasant after three days on the road, that spoke volumes about the type of person he is.

"Additionally, observe very closely how his parents communicate with each other. Those parents were his role models for being an adult, a husband, and a parent. If they are miserable with each other, that dysfunctional behavior will rear its ugly head in some way. Once the luster of romance has worn down a bit over the years, honesty, patience, and kindness go a long way toward happily ever after."

TAKING THE INITIATIVE PAYS OFF:
NINA AND AIDAN

Nina and Aidan have been married eight years and are still madly in love. Theirs is a great story for anyone debating about picking up the phone to reach out to reconnect with someone.

When Nina and Aidan were fourteen years old, they met through his best friend at the time, Sean. Nina had a crush on Sean and wanted to be around him. That was where Aidan came into the picture. The three of them would go to the movies or local diner for fries with melted mozzarella cheese. Sean had a steady girlfriend from camp who lived in another town, so Nina thought she had a chance with him. Aidan also had a steady girlfriend, so he wasn't available, and Nina was pretty sure he didn't view her as a "girlfriend" type, anyway. She was wrong, and ten years later found out the truth.

She recalled writing in her junior high school diary that she started thinking Aidan was cute. He had taken her into the city by train for the very first time when they were fifteen, and she enjoyed the time they spent together. Nina started to forget about Sean and began to look at Aidan in a totally different way. But because he was seeing someone else, it just fizzled out in a friendly way.

Over the years, they tried to reconnect, but Aidan was still seeing the same girl. He'd pass by Nina's house and want to stop in. He'd find himself looking for her car to see if she might be home. She, in return, ventured over to his house one day while they were in college, but he wasn't home. He was at a college mixer with his then-girlfriend.

Coincidentally, Nina was dating Aidan's brother-in-law's best friend (she had met him waiting for a train on the Long Island Railroad platform), when Aidan's name came up in conversation. Since she was not in a healthy relationship at the time, Nina decided to look up Aidan's number in her junior high school phone book (he was living at home at the time). She called him, and the rest is history.

They dated for a year and two months, and Aidan proposed on Mother's Day in front of 1,400 people at an Anthony Robbins seminar in Virginia. Nina was there because she had just quit her job and was hoping to gain the motivation to start a new chapter in her life. He decided to fly to the seminar to surprise her.

When Nina's name was announced and she was asked to come up onstage, the audience shouted, "Turn around! Turn around!" But in all the clamor, Nina couldn't hear what they were saying. Finally, when she did turn around, there was Aidan in a suit, with a dozen long-stemmed roses and his sister's engagement ring. (He didn't have the ring he ultimately gave Nina at the time, so he asked his sister for hers.)

Aidan got down on one knee and proposed before a roaring crowd. "The Greatest Love of All" by Whitney Houston was played in the background, and then "Unchained Melody," which became the first song they danced to at their wedding. The audience was so excited that people formed a receiving line to shake their hands as they exited the stage.

Aidan's goal was to make a lasting impression, and he certainly did that with his proposal. They now have two young children and live in New York City.

MORAL OF THE STORY

If it's meant to be, a mensch will find his way back to you. Sometimes it's just a matter of timing. You have made a love connection, but for whatever reason, it's not meant to work out that very moment. However, persistence can pay off. If you continue to think about someone and feel like he's the love that got away, you owe it to yourself to give it a shot. Don't presume that the other person knows you're interested. He may not, and if you stand on ceremony, no one will make a move. Consider picking up the phone.

Chapter 5 | *Accept Cloud Eight*

We've all been brought up on the dream of cloud nine: Don't settle for less than Mr. Right—or, in this case, Mr. Perfect. But Mr. Right Mensch may be the far better mate, even if he's not a perfect ten. So in this chapter, I'm going to show you why it's smart to accept cloud eight instead. But first, let's talk some more about how important it is to keep your search for the mensch of your dreams in perspective, and to keep not just a realistic but a positive attitude.

Don't Get Manic over Mensch-Hunting

Finding a mensch does not happen overnight, but he is worth waiting for. Until then, as I've shown in previous chapters, you want to live a fulfilling life so you'll be all the more appealing to a mensch.

Remember the story of Ron that I told on page 50? He was my potential MRM. If you recall, because I was so hurt after our breakup, I jumped back onto the socializing bandwagon with lightning speed, seriously pounding the pavement. In an effort to replace him in my heart sooner rather than later, I took an over anxious approach to socializing. I was going out three or four nights a week, whether I wanted to or not, with or without friends.

It felt like a positive tactic, but I experienced burnout. Every guy I met I compared with my ex, and no one fit the bill. How could anyone measure up when I wasn't giving him a real chance by getting to know him? I didn't have the history with anyone else that I had with Ron, but a history—and the familiarity that comes with it—doesn't develop overnight. Even though I knew that, I wasn't thinking rationally enough at the time.

My point is this: Getting manic over mensch-hunting does not mean you'll meet anyone any sooner. Pace yourself, and be gentle with yourself. Try to get over the "What If" syndrome, as in "What if I don't go out tonight? I could be missing the opportunity to meet my MRM!" No reason to give yourself a guilt trip every time you haven't gone out to socialize because you might have missed an opportunity to meet "the one." You will drive yourself crazy and wind up making the rounds in vain.

LESSONS FROM THE LOVE COACH

The worst thing you can do is think that each time you go out may be the last, because "tonight will be the night." That could very well be true, but you may also be setting yourself up for a fall. Things happen when they're meant to, including love connections, though that can be a hard concept to grasp when you're in waiting mode. Instead, before you set out, tell yourself you're going to have a wonderful time. And then do it!

Socializing every night of the week won't necessarily expedite the process of finding your MRM. It's like being on a game show and having the opportunity to choose from doors A, B, and C. No matter what you decide to do, you may always wonder what was behind the other doors and if they might have served you better. But life is not a Chinese menu. We have to make choices and live with them. So don't beat yourself up for your decision to go out or not. Just be sure to really enjoy it, because if you're attaching guilt to it by questioning what you're missing, then what's the point?

Look on the Positive Side: The Hourglass Is Half-Full

As the sands of time flow through the hourglass, it becomes evident at some point that they have reached midway. Does the hourglass then become half-empty or half-full, in your eyes? A negative person would say it's half empty.

Test yourself. Get a small hourglass; you can typically find one that is used as an egg timer in a kitchen or cooking store. What is your reaction as you see the sand pour through it?

Nobody wants to be with someone who has a poor outlook on life and carries the weight of the world on her shoulders. We all face challenges, and life, at times, certainly isn't easy. We have our share of disappointments, losses, frustrations, etc., and some people, it seems, have more than others, for whatever reason. It's all about how you deal with them and your outlook at the end of the day.

Ginny Ehrlich-Greenberg, married six and a half years: "Someone who is not a mensch is still a little boy, and a woman should have only her own children to raise and worry about, not her husband. Otherwise, a woman winds up mothering her husband, and that should not be her role. There should be more of a partnership/friendship dynamic in a marriage. If you want to marry a mensch, don't panic. Be persistent, be optimistic, and try your best to enjoy life and friends, even when you are not with someone. That's why when you are least expecting it, you meet Mr. Right Mensch."

The Half-Empty Glass: Mel's Story

One of my love-coaching clients, Mel, thirty-five, truly perceived his life as if he had been shortchanged. He often compared himself with others, even friends, to see how he measured up professionally. Were they earning more money than he was? Were their jobs more prestigious? Did they live in a better apartment or neighborhood?

Mel's comparisons were really beside the point. Even if some of this were true, did it ultimately make them happier than he was? He would have said yes, and that was the sad part. Because until you walk in other people's shoes, you can't be certain of how they feel and what challenges they face.

We all have "inner demons" that can creep up on us if we let them. It's really about what you want for your life and how you choose to handle what is thrown your way. You can be courageous and optimistic or play the role of a victim, always seeking empathy from others. You've heard stories of people who overcome tremendous obstacles, including abusive childhoods and disease. And yet these aren't necessarily the folks who grow up bitter and negative because they want better for themselves.

In Mel's case, he was so used to thinking negatively that he had grown accustomed to feeling sorry for himself, even though he wasn't badly off by any means. He was a good-looking guy with a stable job and a supportive crew of friends. At the age of thirty-five, he wondered when he'd meet Ms. Right. He was an active dater but didn't grasp how his attitude was impacting the future of the relationships.

We talked about what he wanted for his life and what it would take for him to be happy. He acknowledged that his tendency was to view things through dark-colored glasses and that he wanted to change. Since awareness is half the battle, he decided to see a therapist.

Over time, by getting things off his chest and taking suggestions from me in terms of social events to pursue, he met Rochelle, and they now live happily together in the suburbs with their young daughter. Life is good for Mel, and marriage became a viable possibility once he set his mind on positive thinking.

A NOVEL MARRIAGE THE SECOND TIME 'ROUND: DARLENE AND WAYNE

Darlene and Wayne have been married for twenty-six years and were introduced by Darlene's best friend, Ted, who is gay. Ted insisted that she and Wayne go out or he would never speak to her again. Ted knew Wayne because he was photographing an interior design job that Ted had done. Ted found Wayne very attractive, and since he couldn't have him because Wayne was straight, he thought Darlene should meet him. Ted was also convinced that if it worked out, they would have beautiful children.

Darlene and Wayne married nine months after they met. There was never a formal proposal or engagement. They mutually decided that they would tie the knot. It was the second marriage for each, so they readily recognized a good thing. Though their first marriages were short-lived, they had learned from their respective experiences and chose better the second time round. Ted was thrilled, and he was right: They now have a beautiful grown daughter who recently married a mensch herself.

Darlene explains, "It's hard work to stay married this long. There have been times when we both might have thought it was too difficult, but our love, mutual attraction, and respect for each other carried us through. Someone once said that marriage is like a novel, and nothing could be truer. It's an extended narrative filled with romance, conflict, danger, self-discovery, and characters that affect your life in ways you might never expect."

MORAL OF THE STORY
If at first you don't succeed, don't throw in the towel. The second time was the charm for Darlene and Wayne. As long as you learn from your mistakes, it's about growth, not failure, and you can go on to find much happiness. It takes a strong person to end a relationship that isn't working, but it's better than living a life of regret. Your next marriage can be to a mensch, and you'll appreciate him all the more.

Enrich Your Life through Spirituality

Living a full life makes you that much more appealing, and spiritual enlightenment can play an important role. While to some it may feel like they're trying to pass the time before an MRM comes into their life, it can actually lead to personal growth and unexpected learning and excitement.

For example, if much of your life's focus is on meeting someone, maybe you need to give some consideration to what you've been doing for yourself of late. It's easy to get caught up in the daily treadmill of life. Between work, home responsibilities, family, friends, health matters, etc., there isn't always much time left over to devote to achieving inner well-being. Why is this so important? Let me explain.

Spirituality isn't something that comes naturally to everyone, but if you look at it in terms of getting in touch with your soul—your inner desires—it can lead to self-discovery and put you in a better place in terms of learning to trust your gut. Sometimes it takes getting quiet within yourself to truly know what is important to you. If your head is so full of noise and To Do lists (I'm the queen of those), how can you think past it all?

There are many ways to get quiet. You can explore such practices as meditation or yoga, or even listen to soothing music, get a massage, sit by the water or in a park, take a drive to the country—you name it. Whatever you do, it can help you make decisions with greater clarity, and this is particularly valuable when you aren't making the best choices in terms of dating. I've been asked, "How do you know if you are settling or if you're in love?" If you learn to trust your gut, the answer will present itself when you are still and your mind is clear.

How to Expand Your Spiritual Horizons

Taking a class can be another way to expand your spiritual horizons. You might look into venues like the Omega Institute in Rhinebeck, New York, and elsewhere; The Open Center in New York City; Kripalu Center for Yoga and Health in Lenox, Massachusetts, which also has programs across the country; and the Brahma Kumaris World Spiritual Organization, with locations and programs worldwide.

Give thought to studying Kabbalah—ironically, made popular by such contemporary cultural icons as Madonna—or going on a retreat or taking a spa vacation at a place such as Canyon Ranch in the Berkshires and Arizona or the Chopra Center, with various locations. You deserve to feel good during this stage in your life and appreciate the person you have become. You'll also learn how to be a mensch to yourself, and that will make you want to be with Mr. Right Mensch and not opt for someone you know in your gut doesn't deliver.

EXERCISE:
Get in Touch with Your True Self

Faking it doesn't get you anywhere. So, on a page in your Socializing Notebook, make three columns. Label them Passions, What Holds Me Back, and Action. In the first column, list at least five of your passions. Then, check off the ones you actually pursue. In the next column, write down what is holding you back from pursuing each one. In the third column, record specific action steps you might take to make each happen and, if possible, assign a time frame in which you'll try to move forward, even if you're just moving a step at a time.

For example, if you want to learn to paint, perhaps the local high school or community college adult education program offers a course or two you might consider. An action step would be to call up and request a catalog. Another option is to enroll in a course of study via the Internet. If your schedule doesn't permit your spending time in an actual classroom, you can go the virtual route and still have a chance to expand your mind. But remember: If you take a live class, there's a chance you might meet someone who shares your passion!

> *Making the wrong decision is far worse than being alone, and you are capable of having a full, happy life without a spouse.*

The Love Trap

There is such a thing as being in love with love. You've probably heard this before. Who wouldn't want to be in love? It feels great. It's a natural high. Is it the same as cloud nine? Not necessarily. Consider the following:

The time between dates is just as important, if not more so, than the time you are on the date. If, when you're not actually with someone, you find yourself questioning the person's motives and wonder if he'll be true to his word, then what does that tell you about him? Is he a mensch? Would a mensch say something and not deliver, unless extenuating circumstances arose?

You know the answer, yet it's easy to push your gut reaction aside when you want something to be true. You pine for your dream mensch, so your search will be over. That is understandable, but even if you have that cloud nine feeling with this person, do you want to stick around if it's not mutual?

And what if you're hanging on because of what he represents? Security—financial and emotional. You're forty plus and may wonder if anyone else will surface. Maybe this is the first man who wants to marry you, and you're convinced you should go for it. For some, security would be enough . . . but is it for you? If it is, that's fine. Maybe you love him because he's good to you, and that's nothing to sneeze at. Just know yourself, and understand your marital motives.

Age, ideally, should not be a factor. If you've made it to forty plus, you obviously know you can take care of yourself, so why go for a man now who is less than what you've been hoping for? You've waited this long!

Let me stress this point: Making the wrong decision is far worse than being alone, and you are capable of having a full, happy life without a spouse.

Dating the "Band-Aid" Guy

Being alone is hard for some people. It's like having an open wound that can be filled only by the next relationship. That is what I refer to as the Band-Aid Guy. He's the one who comes to the rescue when you're feeling lonely, but you know he's not a keeper. He's more of a convenience. You may continue to date him because it feels better to be with him than no one at all, but it's not entirely fulfilling.

He may be a mensch because he is there for you in your time of need, but is there a connection beyond that? Even a mensch needs to be multidimensional for the relationship to work. You may not always be able to put your finger on what is missing from a person, but you should know when it doesn't ring true if you go with your gut, as I discussed earlier.

So don't date a Band-Aid Guy just to fill an empty space in your social life. If you don't clear away people or projects taking up your time and energy, you won't have space for new individuals or things to enter. It may make you feel vulnerable at the time, but once your MRM comes your way, you'll know it was worth the wait, effort, and anxiety you may have suffered getting to that point.

Meredith Harris, married eleven years: "It wasn't easy to find my husband, and when I did, he had to smash me over the head to let me know he was the one. I hadn't realized at first that I had to break my old dating patterns. I looked back at past relationships and could see that even though the men I dated were very different people, they had a lot of the same qualities—they were unreliable, self-absorbed, etc. I was rarely the priority. Once I decided to date a different kind of guy, I ended up marrying him. He turned out to be so much more than I ever thought I'd be lucky enough to find.

"If you want to marry a mensch, throw away your lists. Don't confuse lust with love when you meet someone you are initially attracted to. If he makes you his priority, and you feel happy when you are together and apart, that is the person who deserves your time. Even better is when you develop a friendship first, as the rockets will come later and last a lot longer than those based on infatuation.

"So many women date irresponsible men and misinterpret their frustration for longing. Some also make excuses for men not living up to what they could be. You need to ask yourself, are you really in love with the person or his potential? Potential isn't based on reality. You want to stay grounded and evaluate what keeps you in an unsatisfying relationship, and make a concerted effort to find a better partner for the long run.

"Marrying a mensch has major benefits. He is concerned with your happiness. He will be there when times are rough. He will support you. Most importantly, you will be able to trust him. These are the building blocks for a strong relationship that will grow and survive. As time goes on, you will love him even more."

GIVE HAND-ME-OVERS A CHANCE:
LORI AND DAVE

Lori and Dave owe it all to a hand-me-over. That is to say, Dave had gone on a date with a friend of Lori's. The friend, Yael, had been introduced to Dave by a female friend of his. He called and the two met for dinner. Despite a pleasant evening, the date was less than stellar for either of them, but it was the door opener for a relationship that would change Dave's life.

Yael sized Dave up. While sparks didn't fly, she could see he was bright and charming. He possessed a positive self-image, and, most importantly, he had the mensch factor. So how could she let an eligible, desirable mensch go? She decided it would be great to introduce him to one of her friends.

Yael thought of Lori, gave Dave her number, and he called her the next week. After the first conversation, Dave asked if he could take her to lunch. Their first meeting went well, and Lori suggested he give her a call. The next several weeks, their schedules conflicted, but they continued to speak on the phone. Finally, a second date, third, fourth, etc., resulted, and after six months, Dave proposed on the coldest day of the year, beneath a gray sky, on a snow-covered beach.

Each had dated their share of people over the years, and since they were in their forties, both were very clear about what they were looking for . . . and not looking for. They found in each other a recognition of common needs, desires, beliefs, and morals, and spent many evenings talking and listening. They knew it was right when they agreed to disagree. It felt natural for them to be together.

Lori and Dave have now been happily married for three years and have a young child. According to Lori, "Dave is a mensch because he considers the needs of others before his own. He is a concerned and spiritual human being who has his priorities in order. He knows that there are greater things in life than himself."

MORAL OF THE STORY

Never pass up a hand-me-over. If a good friend or associate approaches you and wants to make an introduction, go for it. What's the worst? You might go on one disappointing date. However, someone else's mismatch might be your mensch. If the person doing the fixing up has a good sense of you, it's always worth pursuing. Sometimes she knows you better than you might know yourself.

Chapter 6 | Create a Mensch-Meeting Plan

Let's begin this chapter by talking about what I like to call the Successful Socializing Triad. The concept of the Successful Socializing Triad is that Attitude, Strategy, and Action go hand in hand in hand. With the right attitude, you can create a socializing strategy that leads to action—the socializing activities you will pursue.

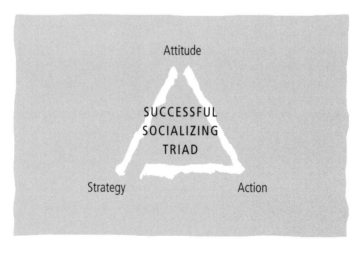

Attitude

SUCCESSFUL
SOCIALIZING
TRIAD

Strategy   Action

I'll discuss Strategy and Action in Chapter 8. And I write about The Three Rights, one of which is Attitude, on page 140. But it bears reinforcing here because, without it, success in the love department may elude you. Attitude sits atop the Successful Socializing Triad, because if you don't have a positive one, not much else matters when you're trying to meet someone.

Now, you might ask yourself, "How can I have a positive attitude if I'm not connecting with anyone?" A key factor is to give yourself a pat on the back for the efforts you are making. It's easy to sit in judgment on yourself and others, and lament what you don't have, but I truly believe that if you want to meet someone and make a genuine effort, it will happen.

You need to possess the confidence to know in your heart that you deserve to meet someone terrific. If you've been disappointed in the past, you may have an inclination to put men down, thinking there's no good one out there. But if you have a downbeat attitude, you will start to believe that mensches don't exist, and that surely won't help you marry one!

The notion of timing can be a hard one to grasp. What makes the timing right? Here's where the faith comes in. Certain things in life we just have to give up to the universe. They are beyond our control, yet a part of us wishes we had a crystal ball to project what will happen and when. Understandably, it might put you at ease if you knew exactly when your MRM would come along, but attracting someone is contingent upon having an upbeat attitude, despite the inevitable frustrations.

Having the right attitude doesn't mean forcing yourself to be happy twenty-four/seven. We all have good and bad days, and you are entitled. You're also entitled to vent. No one is immune to mood swings, and that's part of what friends are for—to be there and help you through it. That's also where a love coach can come in to pump you up so you buy into your own potential for love.

We can never have enough cheerleaders in our life, but sometimes those closest to us don't have the motivation or ability to give it the time. They may be facing their own challenges or have their own reasons for not being in your corner as much as you would hope. They may not feel comfortable talking to you about it. Additionally, if you are negative all the time, no one will want to be around you. After a while, it feels like advice falls on deaf ears if your friends and/or family are trying to offer support but you don't take it. Granted, you may not always want to or be ready to hear what they have to say, but know that they mean well.

All this said, do your best to smile when you're out and about. You'd be surprised how a smile can grow on you, and you just might wind up connecting with someone when you least expect it because your smile caught his eye. He might think you're flirting, and who knows where that can lead?

LESSONS FROM THE LOVE COACH

People have their own approach to socializing, and they get married for all kinds of reasons. Their reasons may not be what you would want for yourself, and that's okay. So, in light of that, you have to make conscious decisions in terms of whom you share your thoughts with, and ideally choose someone who at the very least is a good listener. Sometimes that's all you need. It might just help to vent to someone with empathy, since there isn't always an easy solution to situations, and we know that meeting an MRM takes time.

Define Your Socializing Style

In order to get a better sense of a socializing strategy that would work for you, it helps to define your socializing style. The more you understand yourself, the better this book is able to help you. So read through the social styles that follow and ask yourself which one applies to you. Or perhaps a combination seems most fitting.

- *The Social Adventurer.* You're always up for something new. If your friend hears of a singles bungee-jumping outing, you're there in a heartbeat.
- *The Social Trooper.* You leave no stone unturned when it comes to socializing. You're ready to go out at a moment's notice, rain or shine.
- *The Social Diva.* You love to get dressed up and thrive in a formal socializing setting, like a black-tie event, because you have a chance to show yourself off.
- *The Antisocial Loner.* Your mantra is "I'd rather be at home with a pint of Häagen-Dazs." Socializing is the last thing you enjoy doing, and it's written all over your face (hopefully not your waistline) when you do drag yourself out of the house. You prefer to stay home and wallow.
- *The Queen of Rejection.* You are so quick to judge that you barely give anyone a chance and rarely, if at all, give out your phone number. You're notorious for the catchphrase "Don't call me, I'll call you."
- *The Social Creature of Habit.* You're most content pursuing the same activities over and over again, even if it's not getting you anywhere socially.

- *The Social Scaredy-Pants.* New people scare you because you don't trust them, unless you're introduced. So, even if you make a date, you're inclined to ask a friend to go along or hire a private investigator to check out the guy in advance.
- *The Frenetic Flirt.* All mensches are fair game, and you have no qualms about approaching one or flirting your heart out so they approach you.
- *The Life of the Party.* You have a good time no matter what you do, even if you don't meet anyone. But you often do connect because people love your positive energy.
- *The Social Burnout.* You rarely, if ever, go out, because you're tired of the whole scene.

Socializing Made Simple: Create a Strategic Plan of Action

While I am a big fan of Internet dating, there is something to be said for good old-fashioned, non-high-tech, *tête-à-tête* meeting. I'm not implying that socializing is simple, but from a strategic perspective, it can help to have a plan to follow. One of the first things I do with my love-coaching clients is have them complete a questionnaire reflecting their background, interests, and socializing efforts to date. From that, I create a Personalized Socializing Plan of Action that's unique to each individual. It provides a list of organizations, events, and activities they might pursue. This is their Mensch-Meeting Plan.

If you are unable to work with a love coach, you might create a Mensch-Meeting Plan for yourself. How do you begin? Start by making a list of activities you've pursued to date (or at least over the past year). Include where you've met someone, when the last time was that you pursued that activity, and if you would go again.

If you didn't meet anyone and have gone a number of times, did you not meet anyone because there were far too many women compared with men, or did you just not talk to anyone? This is an important distinction, because it may not be the event itself that was less than stellar but perhaps your attitude or comfort level when you were there. If you find yourself in a state of panic and are seriously compromised when it comes to making conversation in a social setting, you might want to speak with a professional, such as the founder of www.social-anxiety.com, to help you work through it.

Once you've completed your list, take a look at the following socializing options, and see what you'd include in your Plan.

Do Volunteer. This is a particularly good direction to take if you want to meet a mensch. Since mensches are bighearted, they can often be found doing volunteer work for a nonprofit group they embrace. There are different ways to get involved. You can volunteer to serve the cause. You can join a committee to help plan a fundraiser sponsored by the organization, or you can volunteer to work at the event itself. For some suggestions about organizations to consider, visit www.singlevolunteers.org or www.volunteermatch.org, or, in New York, www.singlesforcharities.com. You might also think about a volunteerism trip where you work on projects for the good of the great outdoors, for example. Check out the American Hiking Society, National Audubon Society, Oceanic Society Expeditions, The Nature Conservancy, National Park Service, Passport in Time, or Iron Goat Trail Volunteers.

Play Sports. Most men love sports, so you definitely want to pursue something athletic, even if it means taking a lesson because you're a beginner or lack natural ability. It's the effort that counts. Join a volleyball or tennis league. Check out an organization like www.singlesgolf.com—The American Singles Golf Association, with chapters nationwide.

Enjoy the Outdoors. Check out www.adventuresociety.com, www.northernoutdoors.com, www.wildearthadventures.com, and www.adventurenetwork.com for lots of options in this arena. Organizations like the Sierra Club arrange singles hikes. Another good one is the Appalachian Mountain Club. Consider a fishing trip. An example is Queen of Hearts near San Francisco, www.fishingboat.com. What about sailing lessons? Here's one good school, www.annapolissailing.com. And don't forget about white water rafting, biking, camping, and skiing.

Attend Your High School Reunion or Look Up a Schoolmate. You never know whom you might reconnect with, and now that you're out of your teens, the timing might be right. It worked for Donna Hanover, actress/author/ex-wife of former New York City Mayor Rudy Giuliani, now married to her old high school flame. Don't forget that college reunion, either! Check out www.classmates.com or www.reunion.com.

Attend an Organized Dinner Social. They say the way to a man's heart is through his stomach. True or not? That I don't know, but you might explore dining out through an organized group. For example, The Single Gourmet, or The James Beard Foundation "Greens" (for ages twenty-five to forty in New York), or www.meetatdinner.com (Australia).

Attend a Cultural Event. Now we're talking about singles theater night, gallery openings, film discussions, and the like. I discuss this further on page 128, but one example is www.genart.com for artistic happenings. Some museums host T.G.I.F. parties on Fridays after work.

Pursue Internet Dating. I could write an entire book on this topic alone! In general, I am a big fan of Internet dating, and in particular, if you are a workaholic, you will feel right at home perched at your computer reviewing the options. It is a true socializing method of convenience: You don't have to get dressed or recruit a friend to do it. A number of my clients have met their mensches that way, and I offer a service called "Profiles with Pizzazz," where I help people navigate the Web for dating purposes and work with them to create effective profiles, choose a good photo, etc.

WORDS OF WISDOM

Lynn Harris, married two years: "Mensches are by *definition* the guys you marry, in my humble opinion. Not to create a false distinction between mensches and, say, exciting guys on motorcycles; they can be mensches, too. Not to be flip, but why *would* you commit to a life with someone less than ethical, clueful, and compassionate? There's forgiving, and there's settling. If a guy flakes now and then, you forgive him. Mensches are, after all—and above all—human, not just Robo Nice Guys. If he's great on paper—all Mr. Résumé, the perfect one to parade to your parents—but consistently lets you down, you're settling. Never, ever, worth it!"

SOME INTERNET-DATING SAVVY

Internet dating is a numbers game, and this can be both good and bad. Sure, there are plenty of people to pick from, but where do you start, and how do you keep up with it?

The first thing you want to do is invest in having a good photo taken. If you don't have a friend who can do it for you, there are services like www.singleshots.com that specialize in shooting photos for Internet dating purposes. It's amazing how many clients I've worked with who have come to see me because they haven't had success on the Web.

When I ask to see their photo and their profile, it is typically pretty evident that they either were in a hurry to get up and running or were on the lazy side and thought they could get away with posting a less than stellar photo that they had lying around. I've seen men post photos with their exes (or with their exes literally cut out!) and women post photos with men. I've seen people post photos where you can't see their faces because they're covered up with sunglasses, hats, etc. I've met women with killer curves who don't post a full body shot in addition to a head shot.

Why not put your best foot forward? When you consider that physical attraction is a major factor, and there are so many people on the Web, your photo is the first way you can distinguish yourself, so you don't want to rush it. Choose something that really represents you.

When you are deciding what Web sites to pursue, my best suggestion is to start with just one. I've coached a number of clients who were so anxious to get onto the Web that they felt registering for two or three Web sites was the way to go because they'd meet someone that much sooner. However, what they didn't consider is that they'd have to spend that much more time responding to e-mails or initiating them, including putting forth the effort to review potential candidates on each site.

So stick with one at the start, and choose a Web site that is reputable and has stood the test of time, like a Match.com or JDate.com (for Jewish singles). When you write your profile, it's not meant to be a tell-all. You want to intrigue the reader just enough, and few have the patience to read lengthy essays. This is not the place to post your résumé, as impressive as it may be. Your goal is to be alluring, not to intimidate.

Tone is as important as what you write. You want to catch someone's eye and make him want to read about you. A lighthearted approach is ideal, and specifics are always good. For example, if you like comedy, name your favorite comic or show. Avoid clichéd words like attractive and professional—they don't mean much. Let your personality shine through, and try to have some fun with it!

Remember two things: One, you don't have to date everyone who expresses interest in you; and two, your profile can be changed. So if you notice that you're not attracting the kind of person you are looking for—a mensch—perhaps you need to tweak what you wrote so it appeals to a different type. If you don't know how, ask a friend who really understands you to help or seek out a professional.

Take a Trip. Getting away can do wonders for the spirit, even if it's just for the weekend. Organizations like American Jewish Congress offer singles trips for those under forty and over forty, and I met my husband through Jewish Singles Vacations. If you are Jewish, these are two good options. Cruises can be tricky, since it's much more confining being on a boat, though the right one can be fun. If you're thinking of a weekend, a place like Club Getaway (www.clubgetaway.com) in Kent, Connecticut, offers a good time. It's casual, affordable, sporty, and has lots of theme weekends you can choose from, so there's pretty much something for everyone. I'll talk more about this subject in the next chapter (see page 127).

Write a Personal Ad. Prior to the Internet, personal ads placed in newspapers or magazines were the way to go, and for those who don't have computers, this is still a viable option.

Throw a Singles Soiree. Having a party is a way to take matters into your own hands. One example is a New Blood Party. You get together with friends, and each of you invites a friend of the opposite sex whom they're not dating, and you rent a space or host it at your house. A woman I know told me about a party game she played where each person had to name an appliance that he or she would be and explain why. (She chose a blender.) You might be surprised what this can reveal about a person in a kooky way. Another fun thing to do is hire an astrologer or palm reader. A friend of mine, Leah, works as a tarot-card reader and often attends parties for this purpose. If weather permits, you can arrange a group outing to an outdoor concert. That's always a cool thing to do.

Join a Political Campaign. If you have a favorite local politician or it's time for a major election, volunteering for the cause can be a stimulating way to meet like supporters.

Attend a Unique Kind of Social. Some to explore include:

- www.8minutedating.com
- www.hurrydate.com
- www.lockandkeyparties.com
- www.quietparty.com

Take a Class. Whatever you choose, take something that genuinely interests you, be it wine tasting or welding. If you're signing up just because you think you'll make a love match, that can be tricky. The benefit of taking a class is that if it (ideally) meets more than once, it offers continuity. Continuity can help a lot when you're trying to meet a mensch, because you will see the same faces more than once and have the opportunity to strike up a conversation, even if you don't do it immediately. Some suggestions include:

- The Learning Annex
- Your local high school or community college with an active adult education program
- Colleges in your area that offer classes for noncredit

Sign Up for Dance Lessons. Taking a dance lesson is a great way to connect with someone, even if you both have two left feet. One site you might visit is www.youshouldbedancing.net. There are many dance studios, and if you check your local Yellow Pages, no doubt you will turn up something in your town.

Go to Networking Events or Professional Meetings. Not everything you pursue has to have a singles label. Sometimes professional meetings or networking events can lead to connections, both in terms of business and socially. Check out www.ryze.com and www.meetup.com for networking activities. A great Web site that offers a free e-mail newsletter featuring business-oriented events is http://bernardo.targabot.com. Also check out the chamber of commerce in your town. No doubt it sponsors events and meetings you can attend if you join. Magazines such as *Crain's New*

York Business (and its other regional editions) run a weekly listing of business functions, including offering their own Power Breakfast series that no doubt attracts a bevy of men. Granted, they may not all be eligible, but it takes only one . . . or he may have a friend.

LESSONS FROM THE LOVE COACH

Keep your eyes open! Miscellaneous places like the laundromat, bookstores, bus, airport, a wedding, Starbucks, senior centers, a pool club, Internet café, car dealership, your local Y, your apartment building, standing in line anywhere. . . . Mensches can be found most easily when you're out and about. Keep a smile on your face—and a business or calling card in your pocket!—wherever you go.

Just Show Up Not sure where to start? Visit the Web site www.singlesonthego.com for some ideas. Also, in New York, groups like Social Circles, www.socialcircles.com, have many diverse offerings. All you have to do is sign up, pay, and show up—no planning on your part. There are numerous Web sites that send out free e-mails promoting events that might be of interest. Some good ones to explore, depending on where you are located, are:

- www.bizbash.com
- www.cassworld.com
- www.eventme.com
- www.kinteramasterplanner.com
- www.socialdiary.com

See a Matchmaker. While I'm not the biggest fan of matchmakers, if you really feel strongly about going this route, you might check out It's Just Lunch (www.itsjustlunch.com), as one option. It has many locations.

A Call to Action

If you are serious about marrying a mensch, you need to make a concerted effort by taking specified steps. I have talked a lot about having the right attitude, but this is where the Action part of The Successful Socializing Triad comes in. I suggest that you record your endeavors in your Socializing Notebook, and I strongly recommend that you follow this Plan of Action:

Make a minimum of five calls a week, or send e-mails to get on mailing lists for organizations, events, and activities that interest you. At the beginning, it may seem like a lot to get on the right mailing or e-mail lists, but once you invest the time, you will have a wealth of information sent directly to you, so you won't have to scour loads of publications to decide what activities to pursue. When I work with my love-coaching clients, I give them a list to call or e-mail, including the contact information; you can start with the contacts in "Socializing Made Simple" beginning on page 104.

Confide in a good friend or family member. Share your socializing goals. It helps to have someone on your side who can be there for you during your mensch quest. Ideally, it is somebody you can call if you need a pep talk, want to discuss a date, etc. If it's someone who is married, that might be all the better, because she's not single herself and facing challenges similar to yours, but she does remember what it was like and wants to be there for you.

If you tell her what activities you plan to pursue, knowing you confided in someone can help make you more accountable and less likely to bail out at the last minute in favor of staying home. This is also where a love coach can come in, if you prefer to speak with someone who is in your corner but totally neutral.

Remember, when you identify someone, be aware if this is the kind of person who will be willing to just listen to you or if she has strong opinions to offer. Either way, you want to know what you're getting into and if she's the best person for this role. It shouldn't be someone who will drag you down or be impatient or overly critical, but preferably an upbeat soul who wants all the best for you.

Make Valentine's Day a day of empowerment. Occasions like Valentine's Day and New Year's Eve can be tough if you don't have a date. But, rather than make it a downer, take the time for some self-love. Do something good for yourself. For example, you might book a massage, rent your favorite movie, or order in food and hang out with a close friend. I'm not keen on eating out on these occasions, because they are big couples' nights, but it doesn't mean you can't have fun in other ways.

Socialize at least three times a month. Three times a month is not a lot to ask for. In fact, it's a pretty small amount of time, considering that you really want to meet someone. But I don't want to make you feel overwhelmed and inclined to back off completely. Do not allow yourself to give in! Go out at least three times. It doesn't mean you have to have three dates but that you are putting yourself in an environment where you could meet someone.

Practice self-care. Whether it be meditation, getting a massage, hitting the gym, updating your wardrobe, or getting a new haircut, taking the time for yourself is critical so you can project a positive self-image and be that much more appealing. Make a promise to yourself to exercise at least twice a week, and if you've never meditated, buy a tape or a CD and explore the practice. Invite a friend over and do it together.

While you're at it, take your friend shopping and pick out some new clothes. It can help to get a second opinion. And if you're not good at throwing things away, ask your pal to go through your closet with you. Donate what you are discarding. It can be tough, because we all grow attached to things, but your body and mind will feel refreshed.

Form a Socializing Circle and Nurture Your Friendships

There's a lot to be said for having a strong support system. One way to do it is to create a Socializing Circle. Some people take a similar approach to their professional life. For example, if you are trying to accomplish certain goals and appreciate the insight and experience of others, you might create a Success Team. You would invite a limited number of people, perhaps five, to join the Team.

These would be people whose thinking you respect and who are good at generating ideas, listening, offering words of wisdom, and— most importantly—they understand that you are looking to grow your business or career and want to surround yourself with positive energy to do so. You would meet periodically, perhaps once a month, to chat about where you all are in your pursuits. Barbara Sher, author of *Wishcraft*, and whose work I love, talks a lot about this (www.barbarasher.com).

A Socializing Circle is the same concept. You find other like minds who are single and you get together to discuss your dating efforts, relationship challenges, etc. Unlike a therapy group, a Circle is intended to be empowering, and is *not* a place to share deep psychological issues. It's meant to be constructive, with the concerns expressed, ideally, being applicable to as many as possible. Sometimes you might choose to read a particular relationship book and even use that as the basis for your discussion. There are different ways to approach it.

A Circle, with the right people in it, can be a powerful tool to fuel you forward. It also helps make you accountable, since the people you are regularly meeting may ask you what you've done to socialize in the past month. If you find yourself with little to report, being part of the Circle may motivate you to get out there more.

A Socializing Circle doesn't have to include just your friends, and in fact, it shouldn't. You can ask around or even post a notice on a Web site like www.craigslist.com to recruit participants. You might do a search through www.groups.yahoo.com to see if any already exist online that also get together.

It can be an effective way to meet new people who might offer new insight. Remember, though, that you still want to nurture your friendships. When the day comes that you do meet your MRM—and you will!—you want to maintain a satisfying circle of friends. You can't get everything from one person, and it's good to have your friends to talk to.

Friends Are Keepers

That's one thing I've always made a point of doing. Even when I got married, I never broke off my friendships with pals who were single. To this day, I still have a number of never-married friends. Just because we're in different stages of our lives doesn't mean we no longer connect. I value my friends with all my heart.

I also encourage my husband to spend time with his childhood and college chums. In fact, when I was looking for my mensch, it was important to me that I find someone with friends, and not just buddies he goes to the ball game with, but guys like himself he can openly talk to and confide in. It's not easy for a man to have that, since men tend to be activity-oriented. But I felt that if a guy didn't have friends, then perhaps he was less capable of intimacy, or our relationship would become one of dependency, and that was the last thing I wanted. I also wanted to know that other than family, there were people in his life he cared about and vice versa.

I had heard all kinds of stories of women's getting married and then dumping their single friends, either by choice or because they would say that their husband didn't want them hanging out with them. Needless to say, women who would act like that are not real friends!

Just because you unite as a couple with someone doesn't mean you don't deserve or crave a life of individuality. In fact, it makes you more appealing if you don't rely on your mate to keep you busy or entertained twenty-four/seven. Additionally, if your spouse spends time with his guy friends, he may appreciate you all the more, particularly if they are single. It will remind him of the challenges of singlehood, instead of encouraging him to dream about the life he used to have. For all you know, his friends may be envious and wish they had a wife like you to come home to. We often tend to want what we don't have.

Being with your respective friends can help you both grow and enjoy different experiences that you are then able to bring to your relationship. Plus, a little time apart is good for reigniting romance. So you might want to keep this in mind when you are looking for your MRM. If you are someone who never wants to leave your mensch's side, make sure you're on the same wavelength. When I met my husband on the singles trip I discussed earlier, it was essential to me that he understood that I am someone who appreciates both time alone with him and time with friends. That isn't to say I love him any less, just that I also value the company of others. To me, that is healthy.

Selling Sneakers: Karla's Story

I remember the story of Karla, a friend of my close friend Debbie's. Nothing was more important to Karla than getting married. She and Debbie would go out dancing to meet men, and Karla often left Debbie at the end of the night if she hooked up with someone. There was many an occasion when Debbie found Karla making out in the parking lot with a new guy. It's not that Karla was loose, though it probably looked that way. It wasn't about having a one-night stand. It's really that she was hungry for love and thought that was how she had to behave to get a date, not necessarily a mensch, but a man.

Karla ultimately wound up getting married, and her husband sold sneakers at a flea market every weekend. Karla decided that in order to maintain her marriage, her role was to be by his side as much as possible, so she started selling sneakers with him. She had no time for her friends anymore, and dropped most of them like hot potatoes.

The few times she spoke to Debbie after her wedding, she said she was happy, but Debbie truly wondered, because it was hard for her to understand how someone could walk away from her friends just because she got married. She anticipated that Karla might find herself to be a lonely person one day, should anything happen to her marriage. Hopefully they would have a long, happy life together. And, luckily for Karla, as insecure as she was, she chose a man who liked having her make him her world.

EXERCISE:
What Is Your Dating Belief System?

Check off the sentiments that apply to you and add others as necessary. The objective is to help you become clearer about what might be holding you back. If you get your thoughts, concerns, and fears down on paper, it might help release some of them from your mind so you can move forward. Consider the following. Which ones apply to you?

○ I'm afraid to date because I've been hurt a lot.

○ I don't trust my judgment, since I always pick unavailable men.

○ I shouldn't have to search for someone. If it's meant to be, we'll just meet.

○ Socializing shouldn't be that much work.

○ I resent being rejected if I approach someone.

○ Mensches don't exist, so why bother dating?

○ I can't be happy unless I'm married.

○ Men want only trophy wives, and that's not me.

○ My dad is the übermensch, so no guy could measure up.

○ I'm over forty, so my chances are slim of meeting someone.

○ Men always want sex, but it doesn't mean anything to them.

○ If sparks don't fly on the first date, we're not a match.

○ I can't go out unless a girlfriend goes with me.

○ Love the second time around can't be as good.

○ A man might be an ax murderer if I don't know someone who knows him.

○ Most men are afraid of commitment, so I'll probably never get married.

○ I don't know anyone who's happily married, so why would it be different for me?

119

IT TAKES ONLY ONE MENSCH: KIM AND JON

Kim works as a marketing manager for a natural foods store, and her boss, a while back, gave her a brochure from a nature center where he was executive director. He wanted the store to do something with the center, but Kim temporarily blew off the idea.

A few months later, she was required to go to a mixer held by the local chamber of commerce, and a friend she was chatting with asked if she knew Jon from the nature center. She replied, "No, but I'm supposed to do something with him." They were introduced, and Jon said he was planning an Earth Day Festival and that the store should be involved. The natural foods store became a sponsor and a food vendor, and after the event was over, Jon asked Kim out.

They dated for two and a half years, and then got married. Kim had been an active dater before meeting Jon. In fact, to hear her tell it, she "went through a slew of duds." Out of frustration and a desire for a clean slate, she moved from New York City to the small town where she met Jon, with the hope she'd get away from all the bad choices she'd been making in her life. She had no intention of meeting a man there, let alone the one she would marry. She had made a conscious decision to live in a small retirement community in the middle of nowhere, a place with a small-town feel and affordable housing. Much to her surprise, she met the one single, available guy in the entire area at the time.

Prior to connecting with Jon, Kim had resigned herself to the fact that she was probably going to be alone, and for the first time in her life, she was okay with that. She had good friends and didn't concern herself with meeting anyone who would lead to a relationship. This was in direct opposition to her experience living in New York, where she felt she was always on the lookout for men. While she did attract them, she wasn't meeting quality men.

Kim knew right away that Jon was different. She called a friend, after leaving the event where they met, to see if she knew anything about him. One good thing about living in a small town, according to Kim, is that odds were in her favor of finding out about any skeletons in Jon's closet. No one had anything bad to say about him. She was happy, but scared at the same time, since it meant making herself available for someone. Putting herself in that vulnerable position didn't come easily to Kim, but she felt that if she were ever going to put herself out there, Jon was a great person to take a chance on. She knew in her heart that they had a very strong connection.

Jon is a mensch, and not just to people, according to Kim. He does wildlife rescue and rehab and has become known in their town as "Nature Jon." He's a savior to animals and adores children as well. Until meeting Jon, Kim had been afraid of commitment and dated one unavailable guy after another. She now admits that at the time, she would blame the man for the relationship's not working out, because she was unwilling to admit her part in it—that it basically never felt right to her.

With Jon, she knows she married her best friend for life, and she hopes they will start a family together. Having children wasn't high on her list before, but now with Jon, she has an entirely different mind-set. "I know he will be an incredible father. I can't imagine a mensch who wouldn't," says Kim.

MORAL OF THE STORY

It takes only one mensch. This is one of my favorite statements, because it is so totally true. You can be in the most unlikely place, yet somehow manage to meet your MRM. It's funny, because Kim would have met Jon sooner had she listened to her boss, but perhaps for whatever reason, she was meant to meet him through an introduction. Kim had done a lot of soul-searching prior to her move and was fully aware that for a long time she had made bad choices in men. It is that awareness that helped her recognize the goodness in Jon and how he was right for her at this time in her life. When she let go of the feeling of desperation she had often had, love found her when she least expected it. No one was more surprised than Kim herself! It can happen to you, too.

Chapter 7 | *Step Out of Your Comfort Zone*

Are you a creature of habit, and proud of it? Time to shake things up! If you've been pursuing the same activities for the past ten years and they haven't produced your Mr. Right Mensch, you need to find some new pursuits. Breaking old patterns is critical, and a little variety can potentially work wonders for your social life.

Think about what you've always wanted to do, and go for it. Look at what your friends engage in, and see if any of their pursuits interest you. Tag along, if they don't mind.

It's easy to do what you have grown accustomed to, but it's not necessarily an effective way to socialize. Challenge yourself!

Don't Let Your Zip Code Dictate Your Social Life

One of the keys to successful mensch-hunting is to venture beyond your own backyard when looking for love. The right relationship isn't based on convenience, nor should it be. If you limit your search to your local geographic area—particularly within a certain radius—you do yourself a great disservice.

I'm not talking about deliberately pursuing someone out of state, if you can help it, but let's say, for example, you live on Long Island in New York. There's no reason you can't consider going to socials or placing a personal ad in a newspaper that reaches the lower Westchester area of New York. It is not very far, and more than likely, the person has a car, too, since you are both suburbanites. You need to maximize your meeting opportunities, and that means branching out beyond the obvious. If you live outside the city, venture into the city, and vice versa.

In fact, some people don't view GU (geographically undesirable) as a problem at all. True love can rise above someone's place of residence. On the singles trip where I met my husband, another couple met and ultimately married as well. He lived in Boston and she in Arizona. This was not a deterrent to them at all. If anything, it expedited their courtship, because they would spend entire weekends flying back and forth so they could be together. In between, they missed each other so much that they married within the year. Granted, one of them had to relocate, but they knew from the get-go that that would be necessary, so it came as no surprise.

If you are going to consider looking for long-distance love, though, you need to be clear about what you're willing to do. Are you open to a move, or would it be your partner who would do the moving? What about your career? Is it such that you could get a job pretty readily in another town, or is it okay to move without having a job and look when you get there? Perhaps you have ample savings and are in a stable position without the need to seek out immediate employment. Either way, you should know your situation and be clear about it, so that there are no unexpected discrepancies as your dating progresses and commitment becomes a possibility.

If You're Doing, You're Not Desperate

Don't think of anything you might choose to do as desperate. I've worked with singles who have bluntly stated that they refuse to place a personal ad or pursue any activity with a singles label. To do so, to

EXERCISE:
Create an Eggshell Plan

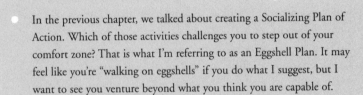

- In the previous chapter, we talked about creating a Socializing Plan of Action. Which of those activities challenges you to step out of your comfort zone? That is what I'm referring to as an Eggshell Plan. It may feel like you're "walking on eggshells" if you do what I suggest, but I want to see you venture beyond what you think you are capable of.

- Once you get yourself on the e-mail or standard mailing lists for those activities and organizations of interest, which ones will you pursue that make you stop and think, "Hmmmm . . . I'm not sure I can do that!"? Don't get scared. You don't have to go skydiving or bungee jumping. But, for example, what about something like comedy improvisation (such as Chicago City Limits in New York or Second City in Chicago) or joining a Toastmasters chapter and giving a talk.

- Does the idea of getting up on a stage and learning to make quick banter or delivering a speech in front of a group make your knees buckle? Then maybe it's exactly what you need to break out of your shell and open yourself up to new ideas that could also lead to a whole new social circle.

- I want you to choose at least one activity that fits this bill, pursue it, and record in your Socializing Notebook how it felt the first time you did it. If you really hate it, choose another and try again. You may love it, come to love it, or simply come to love trying new things! But in any case, you'll grow as a person and a prospective date or mate.

Cindy Block, married eight years: "Don't spend all your time looking for the guy that *looks* right. A mensch doesn't necessarily fit your preset standards. Don't expect it to be someone you're immediately attracted to, either. Maybe it will be the person you have already met a couple of times but didn't consider. It's really a matter of what you want when you're looking for a spouse. If you want a permanent, loving, caring, confident relationship, then choosing a mensch is a must. Being a mensch is a quality that will last a lifetime. All the superficial stuff is meaningless when you're talking about years of a *real-life* relationship. You want the guy who is in it for the long haul—someone who'll be faithful and loving and helpful and caring—that's a mensch.

"Don't judge anyone by anything! If you truly want to marry a mensch, wait to get to know him before you write him off. Looking for a single type of person will get you nowhere. And make sure he's your best friend. When I was single, I was always desperate to have a boyfriend, and therefore, didn't leave a guy until long after I should have. I'd go right from that relationship into dating the next guy, not giving myself much time in between. I had a lot of fun, though, but I thought a couple of guys were Mr. Right Mensch, only to later wake up and smell the coffee. When I was twenty-one, I was engaged, and the day I was supposed to mail out the wedding invitations, I realized it was completely the wrong thing to do. I've never looked back."

them, feels as if they are walking around with the word *loser* stamped on their forehead.

Nothing could be further from the truth. There is nothing wrong with you because you are single. To say so would be the equivalent of saying to a childless married couple that there is a problem with them. Granted, that may be a choice on their part, and you haven't necessarily chosen to be single. But if you are really out there trying to find your mensch, and following some of the advice in this book, then you are being proactive, not desperate, and you will eventually meet your MRM.

If you feel like you are desperate, this might be one of the reasons you haven't connected with someone. No one wants to be with someone who is anxious and out of sorts, so wipe that thought from your mind (and brow). Instead of imagining a negative word on your forehead, how would it feel if it were to say "mensch"? How appealing would that be, both for you and for others? So, presuming you *are* a mensch, be proud of it and work toward connecting with others who appreciate you and your uniqueness.

Desperation is an attitude, but when it comes to taking action, there is no such thing as desperate unless you behave without self-respect. As long as you're true to yourself and what feels right, you will make smart choices, whether you're deciding whom to date or which social event to attend.

Put Yourself Where the Odds Are in Your Favor

Unless you want to marry the reliable FedEx man or that tempting local pizza delivery boy, you have to get out of the house and help fate along. Just as you would if you were actively looking for a new job, you want to follow the game plan you establish for yourself to keep moving toward the goal of meeting a mate. Quality people are often busy people, which makes it harder to find and meet them. This is not to say, however, that they don't exist.

Given the choice of feast or famine, which would you choose? It may sound like a no-brainer, but you'd be surprised how many people don't give this much thought when it comes to finding love. People tend to pursue the activities they know and feel comfortable doing, even if the pickings of potential dates are slim.

This approach is not enough. You need to go where you're

going to find the opposite sex in numbers, and almost no attempt should be perceived as desperate, as I stated earlier. Okay, you might not want to stand on a street corner with a billboard on your back, but you do need to take charge and be a savvy single.

To Find a Mensch, Go Where the Mensches Are

What does that mean, exactly? Consider this: What activities do most men enjoy? Sports. Seem obvious? Maybe so. That said, how can you take advantage of this known fact? You say, "I don't like sports, and I'm not a jock." I hear you; but what about taking a lesson? Golf? Tennis? You might join a league and play volleyball or softball. Some leagues are pretty forgiving if you're not particularly skilled. You can inquire about the level of seriousness of the competition when you explore the options.

What about other outdoor activities? Hiking, biking, whitewater rafting, rollerblading? I'm talking about participation, ideally not spectator sports, though it is certainly possible to meet someone during a tailgate party at a football game or sitting in the stands. I actually once met a guy attending the U.S. Open tennis matches at Flushing Meadows in New York. So you never know . . . but in general, it's best to get involved. You can even volunteer at a sporting event like the New York City Marathon. You'll get a chance to check out the fit men running the race—and maybe even connect with other volunteers in the process.

Something else to consider is travel. I get asked this question often by the clients I coach: How do you find a good trip when so many attract more women than men? That tends to be true, unfortunately, but one way to approach it is to take a more adventurous type of trip. For example, you might go camping in the Berkshires or ride a mule down the Grand Canyon. Check out places like Outward Bound and the Sierra Club.

Here's a big tip: Look at the advertising section in *Men's Journal* magazine. Many travel companies with an adventure bent advertise there, and you know that men are reading the magazine and hopefully taking note of the trips. I often joke and say, if you want to meet a man while traveling, take a "life-threatening" trip. I'm not suggesting that you seriously put your life on the line, and some folks these days are less apt to travel due to world events.

What I *am* suggesting is that if you are planning to go on an organized trip for singles, the trip is more likely to attract men if it's going to the type of place he wouldn't readily visit on his own or with a buddy. For example, places like Israel and Turkey are challenging terrain to navigate, so taking an organized trip is the most feasible way to go. The opposite would be true of a destination like London, particularly since English is spoken and it's easy to get around.

HIT THE BEACH

Here's a good way to meet people: Check out summer-share houses looking for roommates. You may click with your housemates, meet people in other houses, or just have a good time at the beach (or in the mountains, or on the lake). Fast friendships—and happy marriages—have come about in just this way.

Cultivate Cultural Pursuits

What if you're a man looking to meet a woman? Where do you think you'd find the opposite sex in numbers? Sure, you could say the Henri Bendel's cosmetics counter, and if you're good at making small talk about lipstick or perfume, that might not be a bad option for you. But the answer I'm looking for is: cultural activities.

It's always amazing to me: When I lecture and discuss cultural activities, I find again and again that many men don't pursue them.

It's not because they don't have an interest, but often it's something they would do if they were already with a woman. So what does that mean for single culture-loving women? It means that as much as you adore the theater and art galleries, you should continue to go and pursue your passions, but do not rely on it as a way to meet a mensch.

Here's a big tip for men: Several theater companies in New York have singles nights when you can see a show and mingle during intermission and afterward. Some theater and dance companies host fund-raising events that you can pay to attend. There are also places like Festival Chamber Music in New York City where you can listen to beautiful music and have the opportunity to mingle with young professionals in their twenties and thirties. Lincoln Center in New York has a group called Young Friends of Film, where you screen a movie and engage in discussion. (Incidentally, ladies, film is more likely to draw men than other cultural pursuits.) If you live outside New York, look for similar types of activities in your town.

If art is your thing, explore local museums and inquire if they have a young-professionals' group or fund-raising events. Most do, and if you become a member of the museum, you can attend. Check out galleries where you live. A good friend of mine, Adrienne in Chicago, frequents gallery shows that often serve wine and cheese when they open a new exhibition. She has become quite the consummate art gallery–goer, and armed with her business card, she connects with loads of colorful people and keeps a sharp eye out for art-loving mensches. These events are generally free to the public, so it's also a great way to socialize on a budget, as I'll discuss in a minute.

Don't overlook the prospect of taking a dance lesson. Whether it's line dancing, ballroom, or salsa, you can pick up a step or two and practice as you mingle. If you have two left feet, all the more reason this might be advisable for you. You want to be able to dance your first dance with grace at your wedding and shake a mean leg on the conga line as you celebrate becoming a Mrs. Mensch.

Socializing on a Shoestring

Socializing doesn't have to cost a fortune. It's certainly not cheap being single, and dating and looking good comes with a price tag. But, there is a way to approach it more economically.

For example, if you're looking to update your wardrobe, discount chain stores such as T.J. Maxx have excellent prices on clothing, shoes, accessories, and jewelry. There are locations nationwide, and even a Web site from which you can order. Other discount stores like Daffy's, Loehmann's, Annie Sez, Filene's Basement, and Marshalls are also worth checking out. And of course there are designer secondhand shops for that vintage look. So there is no excuse not to look good on a budget!

Doing Good Does You Good

When it comes to places to socialize, sure, dances can get expensive, and fund-raisers aren't cheap. So how about doing volunteer work? I mentioned volunteering in Chapter 6, but it's worth stressing again here. It costs you nothing, and you might connect with some like-minded do-gooders. Mensches would definitely be inclined to do volunteer work, because they put others before themselves.

In New York, there is an organization called New York Cares. It's an umbrella group for a host of nonprofit organizations, and it makes available to members a multitude of opportunities to get involved. You can pick and choose which organization you'd like to serve, and no long-term commitment is required. See if your city has a similar program.

If you are Jewish, there are tons of nonprofits like Jewish

National Fund, Hadassah, and Dorot that host fund-raisers. You can see if they need volunteers to help plan them. In addition, particularly during the holiday season, these organizations often get involved with visiting the elderly, delivering meals, collecting toys for children, etc., and you could help out. It will make you feel good, and you might meet your mensch while being one!

If you're a sports enthusiast, what about contacting an organization like Special Olympics? I did that once when I was single, and it was a lot of fun. It was also an experience that stayed with me in my heart. You can meet other athletic-minded people (not that I especially fit that bill, but I wanted to support the cause), including the athletes themselves, and it is a touching experience—and also exciting—to see the athletes compete. The competition means a great deal to them. Additionally, by focusing on other people, even if just for a day, it gets you out of your own head and can help put things in perspective. When you see the challenges that many face, yours may not seem so great.

Other Free Mensch-Meeting Venues

Other ways to get out and connect with potential mensches without spending any, or very little, money include:

- Dog-walking (I mentioned the benefits of this earlier)
- Hanging out in a park (play Frisbee, and throw it toward your target mensch)
- Attending a lecture at a library or bookstore (particularly if it's by the author of a book for singles)
- Shopping at the supermarket (particularly around the free sample area)
- Sunning at the beach (take a big, colorful blanket)
- Playing on your company's softball team
- Talking to people on the bus, subway, airplane, or railroad

- Serving on jury duty
- Asking for help when you pump gas for your car
- Going to a street fair
- Participating in a charity walkathon
- Volunteering at a telethon
- Joining your local choir
- Acting in community theater
- Frequenting a place of worship
- Attending an art gallery opening
- Going to a public auction
- Doing volunteer work at a hospital
- Teaching an adult ed class or giving a lecture
- Shopping at your local cell phone or electronics store
- Attending a co-op board meeting for your building
- Attending a PTA meeting at your child's school
- Attending a Little League game
- Working at an auto or boat show

Avoid a Tunnel-Vision Approach

What is a tunnel-vision approach? It has nothing to do with driving. Well, actually, in a way it does, in the sense that you are in the driver's seat when it comes to socializing. You control your attitude and the choices you make.

By tunnel-vision approach I'm referring to those who are so specific in what they are looking for in a mate that they limit their opportunities to find someone. We talked earlier about having a checklist and how you want to be realistic about it. What I'm discussing now is your method for socializing versus what you are looking for in a person. You might have a tunnel-vision approach if you are socializing in a limiting fashion. Let me show you what I mean.

Missing Mainstream Opportunities: Larry's Story

I once did a love-coaching consultation with Larry, a young, single Jewish attorney who was looking to meet his female counterpart. His game plan included frequenting Jewish singles dances, placing a personal ad in a Jewish publication, and going on various Jewish singles weekends at hotels in upstate New York.

Initially, it might sound as if Larry were on the right track because he was putting himself where he'd meet Jewish women, right? The problem was that he was encountering the same people over and over again, because he was so precisely focused in his approach. He was pursuing only Jewish activities, because he thought it would help him meet a Jewish woman faster. It wasn't working.

After discussing all that he had been doing, I suggested that Larry consider placing a personal ad in a publication like *New York* magazine. I explained that, while I understood he wanted to meet a Jewish woman, Jewish women read *New York* magazine. In his ad, he would write specifically what he was seeking in terms of religious

WORDS OF WISDOM

June Ross Zeger, married thirty-eight years: "Being married to a mensch is a rewarding life experience. I am lucky to have had my best friend, my love, my protector by my side for this many years. Marrying a mensch yields great comfort and peace. I would suggest that if you leave your windows open, the sunshine comes in. In other words, open yourself up to accepting this kind of human being into your heart. Don't settle for superficiality. If you're out there looking for Mr. Everything, including looks, brawn, intelligence, and sweetness, you need to weigh which qualities would make someone a better soul mate, and those outwardly appearing traits are far less important in the scheme of things."

preference and other qualities. By not considering a mainstream publication like *New York*, he was closing himself off to Jewish women who weren't reading Jewish newspapers or magazines.

Mirror Image: Barbara's Story

More recently, I did a love-coaching consultation with Barbara, who worked in the field of psychology. She wanted to meet another psychologist, because she felt they'd be most compatible. So she sought out professional psychology organizations and attended networking events that would bring her into contact with others in her field. She was convinced this was a smart approach.

The problem was that Barbara had tunnel vision. She had the right idea but was so focused on meeting peers at professional gatherings that she failed to realize what she really needed. I asked her to tell me what she was looking for quality-wise in a person and to write it down for discussion.

It came to light that the best kind of man for her was someone who shared her sensibility, intelligence, and curiosity about the world. These traits could be found in people other than those in the field of psychology. Barbara wasn't looking to discuss psychology per se but thought that in terms of personality, a fellow psychologist would be her best match.

I told Barbara that her MRM might actually be in a totally different profession, and maybe that would give them other interesting things to talk about. Once I explained this, she was able to think in a broader way and open up her dating options considerably. She agreed that she had been limiting her chances of meeting someone and was going to explore attending other business functions for professionals in varying fields.

Men Who Don't Know How to Date Like a Mensch

It's funny. When I tell people that I work as a love coach, a typical response is, "Oh, that must be fun." My reply is, "Gratifying is more the word. I enjoy helping people, and I truly feel I can make a difference." If that weren't my sincere belief, then I wouldn't be doing what I do. However, just when I think I've heard it all, someone surprises me.

I received a call one day from a man named Max, who was in his early thirties. He worked in a field that was male-dominated and thus didn't have a lot of experience with women. He felt that he lacked understanding of the opposite sex and was really struggling to meet people. His most recent "relationship," he explained, had been with a dominatrix. Now, in my book, that wouldn't count, but to him, sadly, he had never really had a true relationship. He came to me looking for advice on his wardrobe, help with conversational skills, and insight into what women want.

It's interesting: With many of my male coaching clients, their challenge isn't so much where to go to meet women but often relates more to doing the right thing. They truly want to behave like a mensch but don't know where to begin.

For example, they're not always sure how to approach someone—what to say, how to keep a conversation going, how to ask for a phone number, how to handle rejection, where to go on the first date, you name it. I find this refreshing and like to share it with my female love-coaching clients, because it shows that men truly do care, but we may be giving them too much credit.

We women assume that men know what to do, and if they're not acting as we'd hope, we reach the conclusion that they're not interested or perhaps just aren't a mensch. However, based on my experience, that's not necessarily the case. Many men really want to date like a mensch but aren't clear what that entails. Because of this, it may lead you to question their motives. If you're in a situation where this might be the case, have a gentle talk with your maybe-mensch and see what he says.

Benefit of the Doubt: Mona's Story

One of my love-coaching clients, Mona, had an interest in Tony, a man at the small gym she went to twice a week. She saw him whenever she was there, and they spoke casually. Some of her gym mates were very prone to gossip, making Mona highly uncomfortable about the prospect of dating someone under their watchful eyes. Mona feared they would taunt her, since they had already made some comments suggesting that she and Tony were a couple because of the vibes they picked up when they saw them talking.

Tony is what I'd refer to as a late bloomer, and so is Mona. Both are in their forties and live at home with their parents. Both are actively involved in their families' lives, helping with aging parents, doing chores, etc. In that way, they have a lot in common. Both are very bighearted. Mona hasn't dated a lot, and neither has Tony, and each is somewhat shy.

One day, Tony helped Mona with some of the exercise equipment at the gym and, in return, Mona agreed to take him out to brunch. As the plans were being made, Mona wondered if Tony would suggest that he pick her up. She also questioned why he didn't say he'd call her to make the arrangements, rather than have her call him.

Ultimately, Tony did drive her to the restaurant and even wound up picking up the tab, because he didn't feel a woman should pay. And while Mona had made the initial phone call to firm up the brunch plans rather than Tony's calling her, she chalked it up to Tony's lack of experience. Rather than judge him for it, she gave him the benefit of the doubt, and she proved to be right.

Tony didn't realize he was sending a mixed signal to Mona by not initiating a phone call. To him, it wasn't a big deal, because it made it easier on him. Now, however, the tables have turned, and it is Tony who is making the calls. He has grown more comfortable over time in the relationship department, and they are enjoying each other's company. Hopefully, things will work out for them in the long run, and Mona will marry her mensch.

Broadcast Your Availability

For some people, this last tactic takes them the farthest outside their comfort zone. But I'm a big believer in letting people know what you are looking for. If it's a new job, ask around. If it's a contact for a project you're working on, network your heart out. If it's a date, broadcast your availability. You never know who will be able to help you.

KISMET REALLY HAPPENS: DIANE AND DON

Diane and Don have, according to Diane, an "ironic sort of kismet story." On a Saturday night, Diane was headed to Chicago (which was driving distance from her home) to attend the premiere of *Plaster Caster,* an independent film a cameraman friend had shot about a female groupie who followed Jimi Hendrix and various rock bands around, taking plaster impressions of their genitalia. (I'm not making this up.) At the last minute, the plans to see the film fell through, and she decided to go to a holiday party instead.

In the meantime, Don was stuck at the Memphis airport, having a tough time getting a flight to Chicago, and was just about ready to fly back to Florida, where he lived. Something, however, told him to keep going forward to Chicago, and he, coincidentally, attended the same holiday party with Stu, his business manager, a longtime friend of Diane's. Stu introduced them, and they spent the remainder of the evening talking to each other.

Diane saw Don again the following Monday, on her way to the camera-man's brother's funeral (the reason the plans had fallen through on the movie premiere). Don and Diane stayed in touch via e-mail and phone calls after that,

When it comes to your social life, I understand this can be a sensitive subject. So you want to choose with discretion whom you share your innermost desires with. In this case, I'm not suggesting you expose your heart, just let a friend know you're seriously looking. This is particularly true if it's a guy friend, since men typically have more men in their social circle and beyond, such as their barber, dentist, and poker pals.

But let's not stop there. Think outside the sphere. Some people are better than others at matchmaking and really enjoy it. A match can come from anywhere. Maybe it's your doorman, personal trainer, or hairstylist. Of course, having "singlehood" in common and eventually got together on a New Year's Eve in Chicago. They've been a couple ever since. They now live in Florida with their infant son.

Diane explains that "Don is a mensch because he embodies the definition of one: someone who is steady, reliable, and has other admirable qualities that make him a good long-term mate. He's also soft-spoken, intelligent, and funny. When he says he's going to do something, he does it." Every morning after breakfast, he turns to her and says, "What can I do for you this morning?" "I still cannot believe I got so lucky!" says Diane.

MORAL OF THE STORY

When fate steps in, there's no stopping it, but you have to put yourself where meeting a mensch might be possible. Diane could have easily stayed in for the evening when her original plans were canceled. Instead, she seized the moment and went to a party where she connected with her Mr. Right Mensch. So don't get down if you have socializing plans that fall through. Everything happens for a reason, and it might be a signal to you that something better is in store elsewhere.

doesn't necessarily make a match, and people aren't always the most discerning, but it's well worth a try.

I know of a couple who met through mutual acquaintances. They had actually gone to college together but knew each other only in passing. Both lived in the same town, and after college, they wound up getting set up by the owner of a local store where each shopped. While reluctant at first, they agreed to a date, and are now married, with four children.

So . . . spread the word!

Chapter 8 | *Learn to Go with the Flow*

The Three Rights

There are three "rights" when you're trying to meet Mr. or Ms. Right, and understanding them is critical to your success. Let's look at the three of them and see what they involve. I'm going to begin with attitude, because without the right one, not much else matters.

Right Attitude

Right Attitude refers to staying positive, keeping an open mind, and being approachable. You give off vibes you might not even be aware of. You want to believe that you *will* meet someone and do your best not to give up (though you don't want to obsess about it, as we've discussed earlier). You may not know how or when or where it will happen, but I truly believe that if you're open-minded and optimistic, it will happen for you. This means giving people a chance and not judging someone in the first five minutes.

If your tendency is to walk into a room, anxiously size up the crowd, and decide in no time flat it's not for you, your attitude could use some adjustment. If you are truly open-minded, you will give someone the opportunity to show his true self through in-depth conversation.

You will also recognize that Mr. Right Mensch might not present himself at the onset. He might be lurking in a corner of the room, in the men's room, or standing in such a way that you don't notice him at first. That doesn't mean he's not there. You might just have to scout around a bit more and more patiently canvass the event or venue before you decide it's time to bolt.

If you rush it, you're doing yourself a disservice. It could be the shy, quiet guy in the corner who is great for you, and maybe it takes your reaching out to him. Perhaps he's scared of rejection. Maybe he presumes no one could be interested in him because of his less-than-stellar relationship track record. You can change all that. You can be the one to boost his confidence, and he can wind up being a terrific catch.

Right Time

Understanding the notion of Right Time is critical to the success of meeting someone and seeing it work out in the long run. You have to want the same thing as the other person at the same time he wants it. This means that if you are ready to meet someone, get married, and potentially have a family, the other person needs to be in the same frame of mind and place in his life.

I don't believe that men, for the most part, rise to the occasion and get serious when they meet someone, so it's unwise to assume that because a guy is dating you, he'll want to get married. If he's not potentially looking for a long-term relationship, it won't happen, despite your level of compatibility. This can be hard to understand, because you may be thinking, "But if he loves me, he won't want to lose me, and he'll propose." Realize this: You can't talk someone into being ready.

Now, of course, if you're willing to live together first, that may lead a man to marriage, but you can't do it indefinitely. Establish from the beginning that you will live together a certain length of time and then get married. But if you have serious doubts and feel that living together will help you make a decision, you are probably wasting your time, because you already know the answer.

Additionally, just because you live together before marriage doesn't mean that your marriage is any more likely to succeed. I've heard of cases where people lived together before marriage, only to wind up divorced. So I'm not advocating this approach. You have to decide, and take the risk if it suits you.

Men, particularly, often need to feel established or settled—whatever that means to them—before they will walk down the aisle. It could reflect where they are in their careers, if they have the money to afford their dream home, if their friends are single or married, if they've been married before, if they're done with their studies, if they've dated a lot, etc. For example, if a man has gone on to graduate school after college, he will need time to enter into the corporate sector and won't be looking for a committed relationship right away, unless you happened to meet in school and have a history. Then things could be different.

It is hard for some men to imagine building a family life of their own if they lack personal stability or fear failure due to a poor relationship track record. You want a man who is secure and happy with himself. Trust me, if he doesn't feel good about his life, the possibility of marriage won't be on his immediate agenda.

Also, if a man is in his forties and never married, this, in my opinion, is a significant red flag. Certainly, there are exceptions. But you have to wonder what he's been up to. Maybe he can't imagine giving up his bachelor pad? That's fine, but then, he's not ever going to commit. If he's a workaholic who's had little time to date but is now ready to make room for a relationship, he could be a promising prospect. On the other hand, if he is a serial-relationship person, meaning that he loves being deeply involved with one woman but never commits, then you know he's not a prospect for the long run.

Some men make you believe that you could be the one because they have good dating manners and genuinely care, but it takes more than that for them to buy the ring. They might not even know themselves what is holding them back. They will probably say that they do want to get married one day, but their behavior doesn't support that statement. They've dated great women, but not one was close to becoming Mrs. Mensch, though many thought they could be the conqueror, so to speak.

Take a look at the person's history. It tells you a lot. What kind of marriage do his parents have? If he's a product of divorce, that could make him gun-shy. And if he has a sibling who is divorced, and whom he saw go through a lot of heartache and endless court dates, that could make him fearful as well. You want to examine how he got to this place in his life. Nothing happens by accident. Wanting a family could make a man walk down the aisle, but you need to make sure it's you he loves and not the prospect of your carrying his child.

The Gun-Shy Guy: Erik's Story

A friend of a friend, Erik is the mensch every woman seems to want to marry. With each relationship, the woman is crazy for him and can't wait to walk down the aisle. Only . . . it never happens.

Erik is in his forties and fits many of the criteria discussed above. While his parents have a good marriage, he has a brother who is divorced. He has a stable career, though he isn't entirely thrilled with the company he works for and probably never will be, yet he's not sending out résumés. He doesn't handle change well and talked for years about getting a larger apartment before he finally did it. Then, he struggled for some time furnishing it.

He's a caring, loyal, generous person and friend, with boyish good looks, who treats women like gold—but they never wind up with the gold band on their finger. Perhaps one day he will settle down, though it's difficult to imagine what it would take for that to happen.

Erik would make a good father, but he doesn't talk about yearning for children, so that won't do it. His close friends are married, and that doesn't seem to influence him, either, as it often does. For now, he remains the happy, confirmed bachelor who will continue to attract women who may be let down by him if they don't take a close look at his dating history.

Right Place

Right Place refers to your choice of socializing avenues. You have to put yourself where you're going to find the opposite sex in quantity. As obvious as this may sound, you may not be doing it. Think about what you're doing to try to meet someone. Are you pursuing exclusively those activities that you know you enjoy, or are you open to trying new things, as I discussed in Chapter 7?

I'm not suggesting just throwing yourself into everything, though. When you start putting a toe into the relationship waters, you have to give consideration to your comfort level. Do you do best attending particular types of events because you are less uptight there? For example, is a small cocktail reception better suited to your personality than a big black-tie event on a cruise ship where you can't get off? It is helpful to do a personality check so you can put yourself where it's most likely you are comfortable enough to potentially connect with someone.

Engaging in a given activity can take the pressure off because you are occupied with what you're doing, and meeting someone becomes icing on the cake. Whether it's participating in group sports, taking a class, doing volunteer work, traveling with a singles group, or signing up for dance lessons, there are countless options, as I've outlined previously. Get yourself out there!

WORDS OF WISDOM

Lois W. Stern, married forty-seven years: "As the old proverb goes, we reap what we sow. Often we attract those similar to ourselves. So if you want to find a mensch, you have to be one yourself. That means you are able to step away from yourself and feel genuine concern for others. Reach out to your friends and family in times of need. But also reach out to celebrate their moments of joy and accomplishment.

"It takes a lot of compassion and selflessness to make a marriage hum along. Life hurls many unexpected circumstances in our path, and we need to be able to weather the bad ones. Sometimes we become stronger when we 'go it' alone, but it sure helps to have someone along for the ride who is willing to listen, offer words of comfort, or even tactfully redirect our line of thought. It's also a bonus to marry someone who occasionally washes a pot or puts out the baked potatoes! And the child who has a mensch father is the luckiest child of all, because he or she learns from that day-by-day living experience."

EXERCISE:
Just Tell Me When It's Going to Happen!

Let's pretend that you have a crystal ball and know that in two months you will meet someone. How would you live your life until then? Take a little quiet time for yourself. Get out your Socializing Notebook, or if you prefer not to write, you can even speak into a tape recorder. Think about how you would spend your time, energy, and thoughts if you knew when you would meet your mate.

Ask yourself these questions, and try to answer as frankly as you can:

- How would it affect your spirits?
- Would it take a load off your mind?
- Would you spend more time doing particular activities?
- Would you focus on yourself more?
- Would you hang out with friends or family and perhaps enjoy it more?
- Would you revisit hobbies you may have abandoned?

As you think about what you've written, you may discover that you'd be a lot happier and your life would be more fulfilling if you were living like that right *now*. Consider giving yourself a break from socializing for the next two months and try to incorporate some of what you wrote in this exercise. Try to imagine the pressure you would take off yourself to meet someone if you knew for sure that it would happen and when. Perhaps if you were able to socialize with a bit more abandon because you knew your single days were numbered, you might be able to proceed with less angst and anxiousness.

We all give off vibes, whether we know it or not, and if you're extremely focused on meeting a mate, this may come across to many of the people you meet and date. They are then placed in a position, emotionally, as if they need to play catch-up to your feelings and intentions, and that is enough to take any fun out of dating. See if relaxing your mind-set helps you socialize differently.

The First Date: Don't Complain or Explain— Just Have Fun!

I get asked a lot about what to discuss on the first date, or even on the phone when you're making the date. If I can stress anything, it's that you don't want to ask for the verbal résumé. It's fine to talk about the work you do, but it's not advisable to grill the other person as if he's on a job interview. Do ask questions, but don't pry. As pressured as a first date can sometimes seem, it will feel all the more tense to the other person if he can't relax and share what comes naturally.

The key is to have fun and see if you genuinely click and want to date again. Don't engage in major discussions about past relationships, especially if it is to complain or explain in graphic detail about how things might have gone wrong. That isn't a turn-on for anyone, though you might feel you're just being candid and sharing. It's way premature for that. What you're doing is airing dirty laundry, and there's nothing sexy about that. Additionally, it's a small world— and you never know if he knows your ex!

> Remember, a date isn't a job interview— don't ask for a résumé!

So what *should* you talk about? Look at it as a chance to bond and show genuine interest. Yes, you should discuss yourself as well, so he gets a sense of you, but it's not your job to sell yourself. You are what you are, and he'll either like you or he won't.

Keep your first date casual and on the shorter side, so you don't worry about the cost or get nervous about running out of things to say. Obviously, going to a movie wouldn't be a great choice, since you can't talk there. Meet in a public place, and arrange your own transportation if you have any concerns about the person or want to be in a position of control. If you don't know what to talk about, go on the Web that day or check out newspaper headlines so you can at least talk about news of the day. It doesn't hurt to sound informed, especially if it helps you keep the discussion on "neutral" ground.

Do not bare your soul or analyze male/female relationships. It's also not the time to get preachy and make the other person feel self-conscious. For example, if you are a vegetarian and try to eat healthy, and your date is a meat-and-potatoes kinda guy, do not impart your strong opinions on how cattle are slaughtered, if you want him to ask you out again. Talk about killing the mood!

Additionally, the first date is not the place to discuss family or health challenges, if you have them. It's not that you're being deceitful . . . it's just too early on. If you haven't talked to your mother in ages, does he really need to know right now? If you're receiving treatment for a medical condition, does it have to be revealed at this very moment? No. There will be plenty of time during follow-up dates or conversations. You don't want him to think you're unstable or looking for free therapy. Show him you know how to laugh.

I also advise that you not lay your cards on the table in terms of what you want in a mate and how you've been hurt in the past. Inevitably, anyone who dates has been hurt at one time or another. It pretty much comes with the territory, and it can even happen on a first date. But don't let it hold you back from trying again! Not everyone is out to hurt you, and most often, it's not deliberate on his part, anyway. If he were truly a mean person, you would not have gone out with him to begin with. We all make choices in life, and while you may not be someone's love match, you can even view the date as a learning experience or "good practice," so to speak, until your *beshert* comes along.

LESSONS FROM THE LOVE COACH

First dates can be tricky if they're fix-ups. Sometimes starter dates don't go well, but you don't want to be too quick to judge. If in doubt, definitely go on a second date and maybe a third. You don't have a whole lot to lose, but don't belabor the situation after that. It's best to move on early before you waste time and get let down by having false expectations that, over time, you might click.

Take the Blinders Off

Don't go through the dating process with blinders on. Women, in particular, have been known to spend endless time trying to figure out if a man likes her or not, when all along, if she only read the signals, she would probably know. Men don't do anything they don't want to do. If he's calling you, it's because he wants to. And if he's *not* calling you, there's a reason. You might not know what the reason is, and while you probably wish you did, in the end, it doesn't really matter. Why? Because you want to be with someone who unquestionably wants to be with you. Ideally, you are so much on his mind that he can't live without you. You rock his world, and he is devoted to you.

It is not too much to have certain expectations of a man once you're in a relationship. He should act like a mensch, and if he truly is one, you will know because he will stand the test of time. He won't be on good behavior just during the courtship phase but always. To a real mensch, consideration comes naturally. While he may not be plugged in to your personal needs right away, he wants to learn and welcomes your sharing with him what he can do to make you happy.

Even during the dating phase, a mensch will know how to behave. What does this mean, exactly? He calls when he says he will. He goes out of his way for you, and you don't have to ask him to. You know you can count on him. He puts you before his friends. He shows concern for your safety. Pleasing you is his priority. He is upfront and honest, and doesn't just fit you into his schedule. He's not hung up on ex-girlfriends and doesn't speak negatively about women in general. If you hadn't dated him, this is someone you could see yourself being friends with. Keep in mind that when you first connect with someone, if he sounds weird, he probably *is* weird, so trust your gut! It will help you pick out the mensches from the masses.

> *Trust your gut to help you pick the mensches from the masses.*

A Tale of Two Cats: Doreen's Story

Consider the story of Doreen and Paul. Doreen was dating Paul for eight months. They were exclusive, and Doreen thought the relationship had serious potential.

A friend of Doreen's was soon getting married, and as a last hurrah, they planned a girls-only vacation for four days at Club Med. Doreen had two cats that she'd had for quite some time, and asked Paul if he could do her the favor of checking on them periodically and making sure they were fed and given fresh water.

Almost from the moment Doreen set foot on the plane, she began questioning whether Paul would follow up as she had asked him to. She thought about it incessantly, including constantly asking the two friends vacationing with her if they thought her cats were okay under the care, or lack thereof, of Paul.

Perhaps you're thinking the same thing I was upon hearing this story. How could she date a man she couldn't even trust to feed her cats while she was gone, after he said he would? Doesn't that make you wonder what kind of husband he would have been if things had progressed?

Fortunately for Doreen, she ultimately met another man, married him, and is very happy. But it took the incident with her cats to make her question Paul's dependability. As it turned out, when she returned home, her cats were fine, and he had done what he'd said he'd do, but the mere fact that she doubted him was enough for her to realize that he wasn't the mensch she was seeking for the long run. They broke up, and she never looked back.

LESSONS FROM THE LOVE COACH

Sometimes it takes strength to leave a relationship, even though you know it's not the best for you. At the time, it may be hard to believe that someone else will come along. You have to keep the faith, because it's only when you open yourself up to the prospect of attracting a new love that you'll have room in your life for it to come to you. If you're caught up with someone else, even though you say you could date someone new, your head isn't totally there.

Don't Be a Repeat Offender

Does this sound like you? Are you a repeat offender? I'm referring to someone who consistently enters into relationships that don't work. She chooses the wrong types of men over and over again. Why? Perhaps it's unknowingly self-sabotage.

Think about it. If this is you, it may be hard to admit. Have you ever dated a mensch? If not, is it possible that subconsciously you're avoiding them? Maybe you think you want to get married, but you really don't. Have you ultimately wound up disappointed with each relationship you've had?

It is important to take note of your dating patterns and not repeat history when it hasn't worked for you. Think about whom you've dated and what was appealing—or not appealing—about them, and be conscious of it as you venture forward.

Legal Issues: Linda's Story

One of my love-coaching clients, Linda, forty-three, had a history of dating attorneys. Three of her relationships in a row were with lawyers, and none of them worked out. Each situation was challenging in its own right, yet all along, she was accepting of the obvious flaws each man had. She thought they could be overcome—no matter what they were.

Linda had lost her father early in life, and ever since, yearned for male companionship. Even though she was close to her mother, whom she loved very much, she had been a daddy's girl, and his loss was deep for her. In an effort to replace him, she pursued relationships with men who gave her a sense of financial security and affection but, when push came to shove, were unable to commit. The good news is that she has moved on. Linda found her MRM and is now happily married . . . and he's an architect!

To Rekindle, or Not to Rekindle?

One obvious way to be a repeat offender is to keep breaking up and getting back together with the same guy. To rekindle, or not to rekindle? This is a million-dollar question, and perhaps something you've asked yourself when you've broken up with someone and were tempted to get back together. Or maybe you've already gotten back together, only to find that things didn't work out yet again the second or third time around.

Rekindling a romance with someone is a tricky scenario. You broke up for a reason. Before jumping back into the arms of your supposed mensch-in-waiting, you need to examine why things ended. Has either one of you changed since the breakup? Was it a timing issue, or problems that you had in your relationship?

If the breakup was abrupt, you may be more inclined to want to rekindle the romance, since you may still have unresolved emotions—potentially, a combination of love and bitterness. It may feel like you can't live without this person, but this might actually relate more to your own sense of loss and vulnerability, since being in the relationship was a "safe" haven from the singles scene.

Don't try to convince yourself that the things you hated the first time around will be any different now. They won't be. And being with the wrong person is worse than being alone. So cut your losses and move on to what you deserve.

If there is a friendship underneath it all that is grounded in trust and genuine love, rekindling may be viable, but you still have to proceed with caution. This would be a good time for some meditation, to see what your gut is telling you.

Re-entering the Dating Scene

Re-entering the dating scene is never easy, but you will survive and even thrive with the right attitude. If you are divorced or widowed, I empathize with how you may feel. Re-entering the dating scene is tough, because you might not have liked it to begin with. Let's face it: How many people *really* like it? And, depending on how and when you previously met your mate, you might not have had to play the field. For example, if you met through a fix-up or in college or on vacation in your twenties, you probably never really dated around much.

If you are widowed and had a good marriage, at least you know that it is possible—that mensches really do exist. But now you are probably thinking that any man will have large shoes to fill. While it is natural to compare future mates with your "original," no two mensches are alike; but you can be happy again with someone new. If you work or have investments, then you are able to support yourself monetarily, so you can choose to remarry for the right reasons. Now that you've evolved as a human being, your next relationship could be even better—or at least as satisfying in its own way.

On the other hand, if you made the wrong decision for whatever reason and didn't marry a mensch, you might be getting down on yourself for the years you spent with that person when you could have been with someone else. There's no reason to go there, though. If you have children, at least you can say that something positive came from the union. Ideally, you learned from your mistake and will now have the opportunity to go forward with greater insight about what you deserve to have in your life. Often, it's through our biggest mistakes that we learn the most. Remember that you can't go back, and you have every reason to be hopeful about the future.

If you are a single parent, I do not recommend taking children on a date until you've had enough dates with the mensch himself and have established that he's receptive. Do feel free to show photos of your children, if appropriate, during a conversation.

WORDS OF WISDOM

Harriet Friedman, married sixty-three years: "I offer the following advice to someone looking for a loving mensch: He has to think you're wonderful—the best thing that ever happened to him. He has to know good stuff when he sees it. He has to not force you into his ways, but be gentle, accepting, and prizing of your friendship. He has to be happy to see you. You need to feel safe in his presence. You need to feel fulfilled. You need to feel the *shock of recognition*—a feeling that you've met before somewhere at some other time—a certain knowing. You need to feel free to be emotionally open with each other, to share how you feel and trust he'll hear your heart. He has to love you enough for the two of you…for better or worse."

COMMUNICATION AND COMMITMENT CONQUER ALL: CAROL AND MIKE

Carol and Mike have been married twice—but not because either was divorced. Theirs is a unique situation. They were married once in a civil ceremony, and then, to please family, were married again in a religious ceremony. You see, Carol had by then completed her Orthodox conversion. Carol was Catholic, and Mike was an Orthodox Jew raised in Israel. When they met and fell in love, it was not a simple situation for either of them or their respective families.

They connected at work, and according to Carol, she met Mike long before it occurred to her that he could be more than just a friend. He was the one who helped her out when she needed it and was funny and sweet when she was down in the dumps. She never expected to be attracted to him. Lucky for her, she was able to recognize his mensch qualities and fall in love with a good thing.

While it took some time to work on resolving their religious differences, it was worth it. They dated for ten months before getting engaged. He proposed in her apartment in a tux with candles and many dozens of roses, on one knee.

To hear Carol tell it, "I didn't consider dating Mike when we first met. I wanted to date the cuter but unreliable guy. I wanted lots of things that looked attractive on the surface. But when it came down to it, I fell in love with the guy who sat with me for four hours when I hurt my shoulder skiing, making me

If your date is a single parent, too, you can compare notes on parenting challenges.

If he has children and you don't, be sure to make it clear that you are open to being a mother to someone else's children (if that is true), if he has custody or shares custody. You want him to know from the outset that motherhood is something you would like. If smile the whole time, and drove me home, quite a distance, because I couldn't drive a stick shift with a sling. He was the one who, even when we weren't dating, would go out of his way to pick me up because he knew I didn't have a car.

"He was always concerned about my welfare . . . making sure I got home safely. He didn't have a lot of money—or a lot of hair, for that matter. But he was all heart: good, honest, reliable, trustworthy, sweet, loving heart. Looking back, a lot of the guys that were attractive on the surface aren't so attractive anymore, for a variety of reasons. Mike is even better than he was when we first married. His goodness, patience, and love have made me a better person."

MORAL OF THE STORY

Though it's a cliché, I can't help but write here: Don't judge a book by its cover. Mike might not have been a picture-perfect mensch physically, but in the grand scheme of things, is that what counts? I hope you know the right answer to that.

And that's not the only lesson here. Take a look at the commitment Carol and Mike were able to make. In order to share their lives, Carol was willing to study an entirely new religion and convert because it was what was necessary to be with Mike. She didn't let it become a hurdle to their love. Through communication, they were able to openly discuss the options and arrive at the approach that worked for them, in order to be together. So it can be done. If your heart is there, and it makes sense, your head will follow.

building a family together is at the top of your agenda, and you'd like to have biological children or adopt, it is important for him to know that. You don't want to wind up wasting time with someone on a different wavelength than you.

Synchronize Your Watches

A common question among my love-coaching clients is, "So what makes a man ready?" They want desperately to get inside the mind of a mensch to understand what it takes to find one ready to walk down the aisle.

Are you asking yourself this question as well? If so, I wish there were a simple answer, but unfortunately, it varies based on the person and his life experiences. On the most basic level, your watches (or inner time clocks) must be synchronized, meaning that you have to want the same thing at the same time—as I discussed earlier, the Right Time. You both need to be in the same time zone, at a place in your lives where you are ready to share with someone else and are excited at that prospect.

You can't imagine life without a mate—in particular, the person you've found—and while marriage feels like a big, scary step, you know you are about to embark on a new life with this person you love. It shouldn't feel like something you have to do, but, rather, taking the leap is a step you long to make because you know it's totally right.

If a man has *un*finished business in his life, he is surely not marriage-ready. Consider the following "*uns*" when you're sizing up a potential mate's readiness to wed:

- *Unsatisfying job:* If he doesn't feel financially secure or content on a professional level, he's not marriage-ready.
- *Unfinished divorce:* This is a no-brainer. Until it's a done deal, he's not marriage-ready.
- *Uninterested in living on his own:* If he still lives at home with his parents (and he's not rushing to introduce you), what makes you so sure he's game to live with you? He's not marriage-ready.

- *Unpolished approach to dating:* If he's still trying to figure out the dos and don'ts of dating, and shows his awkwardness in public, he's not marriage-ready.
- *Untreated bouts of depression:* You're not his therapist. Ideally, he has worked on himself, if need be, before hooking up with you. If he's not in a good emotional place, he's not marriage-ready.
- *Unspoken wants:* Communication is key in a healthy relationship. If he doesn't know how to share his thoughts, feelings, and wants, how are you supposed to know what's on his mind? Dating isn't a guessing game. He's not marriage-ready.
- *Unresolved feelings for an ex:* Rebound relationships typically don't work unless time has passed. If he's still harping on his ex, whether girlfriend or wife, he's not marriage-ready.
- *Underlying jealousy:* Is he truly capable of supporting your endeavors? Is he happy for your achievements, or does it make him question himself? If he's jealous, discontented, or feels like a failure, he's not marriage-ready.
- *Unfocused approach to life:* If he doesn't know what he wants for his future, and never uses the word *we* when discussing it, he's not marriage-ready.
- *Uncontrollable temper:* If he harbors a lot of anger, for whatever reason, you don't want to be the victim of his outbursts. This is especially true if he is in denial about his temper. Unless he gets it under control, he's not marriage-ready.
- *Unreasonable desire for change:* He says he loves you, but can't wait to change you. He's not marriage-ready.
- *Unhealthy relationship with his family:* If he doesn't relate well to his parents or siblings, he may not be fully capable of

entering into your family. He needs to have respect for his potential in-laws. Otherwise, he's not marriage-ready.

- *Uncertainty about committing to one person forever:* It's natural to have some trepidation, but not because he feels he's missing out on other women. If he didn't date or sleep around enough before meeting you, he's not marriage-ready.
- *Unending need to be in control:* It can be as simple as his always needing to choose the movie or restaurant. If his goal is to dictate your lives, with little concern for your feelings, he's not marriage-ready.
- *Unrelenting desire to hang with his guy pals:* If his male buddies come first in his life, and he's not looking to introduce you, he's not marriage-ready.

This is just a sampling. From your experience, if you were to look back at relationships that didn't last, you could probably add to this list. These are all his issues, and not matters that reflect on you in any way. You are not his career counselor, mediator, therapist, sports-bar buddy, etc. It's not your job to figure him out, and if you have to read between the lines because he gives you mixed messages, you are obviously not on the same relationship track.

Actions speak louder than words. Even if your guy talks about marriage, his behavior must echo his sentiments for you to take him seriously. Does he talk about the future and want to include you in plans? Is he ready to put others before himself—namely, you and any children you might have? Can he be exclusive with one woman?

Your MRM should love you for who you are and believe that you can enter the future together, through the good and the bad. If he doesn't, and you're hoping to change him (beyond wardrobe issues, which can be challenging enough!), you are fooling yourself. That's not a good way to enter into marriage.

> *Where a man's intentions*
> *are concerned, actions*
> *speak louder than words.*

Don't Mistake Anxiety for Passion

Just because your heart skips a beat does not mean you are in love. In the beginning, as you get to know someone, it is easy to mistake anxiety for passion. Don't be fooled. How you feel when you're not together is as important as the time you spend together, and it can be an important gauge. If you are feeling loads of anxiety—wondering what he thinks, if he'll call again, if you're compatible, etc., etc.—he may not be the one. When things are meant to work out, the relationship typically flows fairly smoothly. Of course, there can be exceptions, but again, trust your gut.

A Tale of Telephone Love #1: Brenda's Story

One of my love-coaching clients, Brenda, thirty-three, fell in love with a guy before they even met. He answered her personal ad, and they chatted regularly on the phone before getting together. Both had busy schedules, so their first date got put off. Because they had so much phone chemistry, Brenda was convinced that he could be the one.

You can probably guess what happened. When they met, it was a huge letdown. For whatever reason, they didn't click, and that ended things pretty quickly. Brenda realized that she wasn't really in love. She had built up the situation because she was hopeful she wouldn't have to look anymore.

It's always best to make the date and not chat too much on the phone or via e-mail before you meet. Otherwise, it's likely that you've already divulged a great deal, and it's not easy to live up to the level of intimacy you've shared through your written words and conversation, since you're really still strangers.

A Tale of Telephone Love #2: Ruby's Story

Ruby, forty-four, was a young widow with two teenage children. She hadn't dated since her husband passed away, and didn't know how to re-enter the dating scene. She had met her husband through mutual friends, so she was never really out there looking for long.

Ruby decided to try the Internet and signed up for www.jewishmatchmaker.com. She was nervous and excited at the same time. Jack, one of the men who responded to her profile, caught her eye. While they lived in different towns, she actually liked that idea, because she preferred not dating someone others in her town might know. She wasn't keen on gossip.

Because they lived some distance apart, getting together wasn't the easiest, so she gave him her phone number. He called her one Friday night, and they spoke for hours—until 3:00 a.m. Ruby was elated and couldn't wait to arrange a date.

Unfortunately, things got weird after that. In subsequent conversations, Jack talked about other women he was dating and about his experience thus far with jewishmatchmaker. He sounded like a playboy and professional jewishmatchmaker client, and that turned Ruby off. As a result, they never met, and Ruby was hurt and disappointed.

The good news is that Ruby realized she had been overzealous and vowed to try to take more of a low-key approach with future men. She was an Internet dating novice but was quickly learning the relationship ropes.

Don't Be a Bud, Be a Babe!

When you meet someone and you have high hopes for romance, the last thing you want to do is become his best friend—meaning a pal, a buddy or bud—and not leave room for courtship and a little intrigue. Give him the opportunity to show his intentions. Is he really a mensch? How will you know if you don't let him prove it?

A bud makes herself readily available and puts herself out as a buddy would, thinking it's a good thing. You might be asking, "Why not reach out to a love interest, via phone or e-mail? Why not hang with him on a Friday night, even if he calls the night before to make the plans?" Here's why not: Where do you go from there? It's great to feel like you hit it off in such a way that you don't hesitate to reach out to your potential MRM, to chat, share, and support him, but how does this promote romance ?

Let Him Take the Lead: Iris's Story

One of my love-coaching clients, Iris, twenty-eight, often placed herself in this very situation. It was her standard approach to dating.

She thought nothing of calling up a guy after a date to talk up a storm, and even if they took turns calling each other, she was okay with the fact that she was just as much the initiator as he was.

After maintaining this behavior for a number of months, and not seeing a relationship progress, she would question why things weren't working out, but it never occurred to her that a contributing factor was likely her own behavior. She wasn't able to get a clear read on the guy, because she didn't permit him to be the pursuer. Most mensches prefer to be in that role. While it is flattering and takes the pressure off a man if you are calling him, the end result may not

EXERCISE:
Read the Relationship Tea Leaves

There are always signs in a relationship that you may or may not choose to see. It's time for a serious reality check! Think about the men you've dated in the past and any you may currently be seeing. Get out your Socializing Notebook and make three columns across a sheet of paper: Red Flags, Time Frame, What Do I Want from Him?

- Write down the names of the guys you're taking a look at. Then, in the first (Red Flags) column, list what comes to mind in terms of things that have raised a red flag as far as your dating them.

- In the second (Time Frame) column, write down how long you will give the relationship (or how long you did give it, if it's over). For example, are you willing to give someone three to six months, if he is unhappy with his job, to rewrite his résumé and make a serious effort to find a new one?

- In the third (What Do I Want) column, write down what you want from this person. Do you want a future with him? Or is he a "boy toy" for now, so you can live with the red flags you've identified?

I promise, after you've finished this exercise, it will be clear in your mind where you are (or were) with everyone on the list!

be to your liking. No guy wants to know from day one that he has a sure thing.

How to Go from Bud to Babe

Be a babe—and a busy one. Be the woman he longs for. Seduce him with uncertainty, not just your looks. Make him come back for more. Let him wonder a little and know what it feels like to crave your company and not know for sure he can count on it. Allow him to miss you by not accepting his every invitation, as hard as this may be.

Demonstrate that you have a life you love. Show him you're looking for the real deal, and don't hang on his every word or be overly impressed with obvious gestures he might make. He needs to prove himself a lot more than by giving flowers or candy—though that's a nice start.

A bud also tends to allow herself to be a "dumping ground," so to speak. She becomes the listener and almost quasitherapist, if the guy talks about his life challenges—anything from his disappointing job situation to his losing his hair. If you find that men often share too much with you from the beginning, and it feels like information overload, perhaps you are somehow inviting this type of discussion without realizing it. Maybe they sense that you'd be receptive to it. Do you, deep down, relish the idea of "saving" or advising someone?

Now, you might be thinking, "But I want to be his best friend . . . a staunch supporter. Isn't that a good basis for a relationship?" In the long run, yes, it is. But it needs to develop over time. If you start out as friends and are really there for each other, it is possible to transition to more. But if the friend or confidante part is overwhelming while you are actively dating, you may never become lovers who stand the test of time.

Sure, you may become sexually intimate, but that doesn't promise a commitment, especially on the guy's part. Most men are very capable of enjoying a sexual relationship without buying the wedding ring. Since we are speaking of marrying a mensch, we would hope that he might be different, but mensches have libidos, too. He may make it clear to you that he enjoys the sex and appreciates you but isn't looking to settle down. In that case, you may respect his honesty, but where does it leave you, if your goal is marriage? As I said earlier, I have a three-month *shtup* (sex) rule, if it is marriage that you seek.

Before you bare your soul or body, give serious consideration to what you want from the person you are dating. Don't kid yourself. Decide if this is someone you could see yourself marrying. If so, then work on letting out the babe in you. Back-burner the bud approach and save it for someone whose company you enjoy for now, but whom you don't see as marriage material. It's okay if you're both on the same page, but if your ultimate goal is to get a mensch to "close the deal" with a ring, you don't want to waste too much time chilling with men who aren't serious prospects. Oh, yes—*never* be the first to say "I love you." Let the mensch take the lead!

My mom always said, "You chase a man until he catches you," meaning that you act just interested enough to whet his appetite so that he becomes the pursuer. This is smart advice . . . and my mom married a mensch. So think like a catch, and hopefully you'll soon feel like one!

EXERCISE:
Why Do You Want to Get Married?

It's time to get out your Socializing Notebook again. Make three columns. In one, list all the reasons you want to get married. In the second, corresponding to the items in the first column, note by each listing if it's something you could achieve on your own. Do you need a man to make it possible? If not, then in the third column, write down what it would take for you to achieve what you listed in column one.

I'd also like you to give some thought to what marriage means to you. Have you dreamed of getting married since you were a little girl? What did you think back then that marriage would be like, and what is your perception of it now?

The goal of this exercise is to raise your level of awareness regarding your reasons for wanting to get married, and to encourage you to believe that you are more capable than you know when it comes to doing certain things for yourself. Believing that should make you feel more self-assured and inclined to opt for marriage for the right reasons, as the stories in this chapter illustrate.

Marriage is a great state of being, but only when you make the best choice for yourself. The challenge is to be married and happy. Anyone can walk down the aisle and be Cinderella for a day. Make sure you're Cinderella for a lifetime!

LOVE KNOWS NO AGE: LEE AND ALLAN

Lee and Allan have been married for thirty-three years and have two grown children. They met at a Bungalow Colony in upstate New York. In Lee's words, "I went to visit a friend at the Bungalow Colony, and when a guy I thought was my friend walked by me, it seemed odd, because he didn't acknowledge me. I turned and asked, 'What's the matter, Steve—you can't say hello?'

"With that, he turned and said, 'I'm not Steve.' The resemblance was uncanny. He looked *exactly* like my friend Steve. I was immediately attracted to him, and told another person I wanted to meet him. After watching him work behind the grill at the luncheonette all weekend and asking everyone about him, I knew I had to go out with him. I even told my friend, 'I'm going to marry that guy someday.' When I returned home from the weekend trip, I informed my mom that I had met someone I was going to marry. I was that sure.

"It was a defining moment for me in my life, because at that point, I was hanging out with the wrong people and had just set my sights on meeting new people. It proves that when you want to change your life, you have to go out and make it happen. Most people just sit back and wait for things to come to them.

"Although I got married very young (at nineteen), I was fortunate enough to marry my best friend. I got a lot of comments from friends that I was too young to settle down, that I should go out and meet more people. My parents knew that I was young, but they were from a generation where that wasn't uncommon. Allan and I both agreed that in order to be together, we would have to get married out of respect for our parents. Living together, at the time, wasn't the right thing to do.

"There are ups and downs in a marriage, as with everything in life, but if you have the utmost respect for each other, it truly works. Most important, laughter! A mensch is a person who is your friend first . . . someone who treats you with respect . . . someone who has empathy and is nonjudgmental. They think of the little things that would make you happy, make you laugh, and make your life easier . . . in other words, a *real person!*"

MORAL OF THE STORY

Some people just know when they've met the right one, even at a very young age. It's often an unexplainable feeling—like you've known this person a lifetime, even though you just met. As a teenager, Lee knew that Allan was her soul mate, and she was right. You can't listen to what others have to say and be affected by their opinion. You have only one life to lead, and you deserve to be happy and follow the path that calls out to you. If you feel you've met your mensch soul mate, go for it. It would be far worse to live a life of regret and constantly think of the one who got away.

Chapter 9 | A Ten-Step Program for Menschmating

In this chapter, I want to sum up some of the key points I've made in this book, with the hope that they stick with you. Believe me, based on my experience coaching hundreds of people, it's the very best advice I can offer!

As a reminder, you might actually want to write down these points in your Socializing Notebook, so that you have them in the same place as your notes. Otherwise, consider making a Xerox of this chapter and put it into your notebook for posterity.

Hopefully, the day will come when you look back on it and realize that you are now with your MRM because you've overcome some of the challenges you've faced, and have learned about yourself in the process. That is what I wish for you. So go forth and date with gusto . . . and remember that Mr. Right Mensch is probably looking for you, too. I have every faith that you will one day succeed in finding your *beshert* (soul mate)—the one you're predestined to be with—*if* you follow the advice I've outlined in this book.

Let's take a look at the ten steps:

Step #1: Don't Judge Yourself or Others

Looking for a mate is the best time to befriend yourself. *You* need to like you before someone else will! Is there emotional baggage that you are carrying from other relationships, or even from the relationship you have or had with your parents? Do your parents make you feel good about yourself, or do you feel judged? What was it like for you growing up in their household? Do you still live at home and follow their rules? Do you have friends who are supportive, or do you feel competitive with them?

Now's a good time to take stock of your life and see who's in it and how they influence you. On a subconscious level, you might be affected by others, but you are so used to it that you don't realize the impact it has, both in terms of self-esteem and in the choices you make.

It has been said that sometimes we choose mates who help us complete, or at least tackle, the unfinished business we had with our parents. They can help us face our demons, so to speak, and rise above by acknowledging and confronting them head-on. Of course, this doesn't happen overnight, but with a mensch by your side, it becomes a viable possibility.

If your answers to most of the questions I've posed above were negative, I implore you to work on your confidence before you seriously embark on a mensch quest. It's hard enough to stop ourselves from self-judgment. Everyone has insecurities. But if this leads you to judge others, you are more likely to pass up a prime mensch and not even know it.

It is so easy to jump to conclusions. None of us likes to be viewed superficially. We want someone to get to know us, yet it is very tempting, especially since many of us are in so much of a hurry, to size up people using the same standards we resent being judged by—for example, looks.

Your initial reaction isn't always indicative of the possibility this person presents. It takes time to get to know the very core of a person. You look for chemistry, but sometimes it's not there right away. That doesn't mean it won't develop if you can get past the facade. No one, not even Brad Pitt, became a megastar overnight, and as hunky as he is, he wound up divorced from Jennifer Aniston.

Step #2: Take Risks and Break Old Patterns

Jumping off a cliff or swimming with sharks may not be your thing. My friend Fran is the supreme adventurer, but I don't know many like her. She is always looking for exciting challenges, many of which are risky. But she does her homework so she can pursue them as smartly and safely as possible. She even writes books on the subject so others can follow in her daring footsteps.

We should try to bring out just a little bit of the Fran in us, because if we don't, it's so easy to get stuck in a rut. Life can become routine after a while, if we let it. There is something comforting about that, on one hand, because we think we know what to expect. But what we expect becomes dull vs. dullsville if it's always the same thing. So shake things up! Don't let all your socializing endeavors feel like carbon copies, or your life will become a bore.

Taking the Bull by the Horns: Michelle's Story

My friend Michelle is such an inspiration. Single and in her thirties, she hasn't been content with her life of late. Actually, she'd thought that for a while but recently took the bull by the horns. She knew that she wasn't meeting her MRM readily in her town, and her job wasn't thrilling her anymore. She liked her work as a therapist but wanted to work elsewhere. So she decided to put her house up for sale, and, shockingly, got a buyer within days . . . much quicker than she ever anticipated.

Luckily, Michelle had been sending out résumés and received a call from a potential employer in another town. She drove down with her two dogs in tow, left them with her mom, and went on a job interview. They made her an offer, which she accepted without hesitation and, amazingly, shortly thereafter found a new house in the town where she would be working. She loved the new house even more than her old home. It is near the beach, a place that she has always adored.

While Michelle is on the verge of leaving behind all that she has known, she is thrilled because it's an opportunity to discover the good that can lie ahead for her. It all happened so quickly that her head is spinning, yet she knows that it is *so* the right course of action. The pieces fell into place, but only after she got the ball rolling. Additionally, the town she is moving to is chock-full of other young professionals, so it's likely that she'll take the local mensches by storm once she gets settled.

You might be thinking, "*I* could never do that—change my life that way!" But you'd be surprised what you are capable of if you put aside your fears. You don't have to embark on a major move, but breaking old patterns means trying things you haven't pursued in the past. It can be as simple as commuting a different way to work or going out in a different town. I've read about the exercise of brushing your teeth with the hand you don't typically use, just to break the old pattern. Granted, this won't do much for your social life, but you get what I'm saying.

Step #3: Know That Every Day Is a New Opportunity

You may have heard the saying "Yesterday is history. Tomorrow is a mystery. Today is a present." I love this, because it really makes you stop and think.

There is no point to living in the past or dwelling on it. We've all had disappointments, but we grow as we learn from them and don't wallow in them. You have my permission to wallow a little . . . but time's up! You're moving on, starting today. We can't change decisions we've made or time we've spent, perhaps with the wrong people or no people at all, but you're reading this book, so you're poised for socializing success if you make the effort.

While we are unable to predict the future, tomorrow can be the start of the love life you've been longing for. You might meet your MRM, or come that much closer to him. Decide today that you're going to do whatever it takes to relate to new people. Doing little things daily can bring you that much closer to your marital goal. Stick to your Socializing Plan. It's amazing what can happen in a twenty-four-hour period! Life can become exciting, even if you don't meet your mensch tomorrow. The more you believe that he exists, the more likely you are to connect, because you are putting out positive vibes.

Step #4: Accept Cloud Eight

Don't have your head so high in the clouds that you don't recognize a potential Mr. Right Mensch when you see one! You can read all about the importance of being willing to accept cloud eight in Chapter 5, but just as a reminder of how we set ourselves up for failure by demanding cloud nine, here is Alyse's story.

A "Class"-ic Case: Alyse's Story

One of my love-coaching clients, Alyse, shared with me her recent heartbreak. She had developed a crush on a man in her grad school class who helped her with a paper she had to write. To show her gratitude, she wanted to give him money or send a gift certificate; but while discussing it with him, the idea of having wine and cheese after class came up, and he agreed. Alyse was thrilled, thinking that now there might be an opportunity for her to explore a potential romance with him.

While the outing was pleasant enough, she couldn't read his interest. He didn't give her any clear indication of wanting to date her, yet she knew that he was shy and was coming off a broken engagement. When she next saw him in class, he didn't have much to say to her. It felt awkward.

Alyse struggled to make sense of the situation . . . especially because she had thought he was a mensch, but now she wondered if perhaps he was proving otherwise. Had her judgment been off? How did she really know he was a mensch? Why did he not want to date her? Could they be friends?

The truth is that Alyse had set herself up for a fall. She had high expectations of their drinks together and was flying on cloud nine before they even went out. She had convinced herself that he was her MRM and that she was in love. From what she had seen of him in class, she was sure that he was a mensch and that maybe one day they would make it to the chuppah.

I reminded her that she really didn't know him. What she loved was her perception of him and what he represented to her, though he hadn't proved himself in any way, other than once helping with an assignment.

So I urge you, as I explained to Alyse, to consider cloud eight when you are looking for your mensch. It doesn't mean that you will love him any less, just that you're not hung up on how you think love should feel to the extent that it keeps you from connecting with someone who in the long run has the power to make you *very* happy.

Step #5: Get That New Do!

A physical change like a flattering new hairdo can do wonders for your self-esteem. But the change doesn't have to be physical. The point is to spur yourself into some kind of action that is a departure from the past.

My friend Mindy told me recently that despite her very hectic schedule as a successful interior designer and media personality, she decided to take up racquetball. She didn't know much about the game, but a new gym near her home opened with courts, so she looked into learning how to play. Now, in an effort to get more physically fit beyond her regular workout, she plays once a week and is loving it.

Not only is it a great sport but Mindy is meeting new men and women partners to play with and, without much effort, is cultivating a larger social circle. For all she knows, she may meet a racquet-ball-playing mensch at the court any day. But, whatever happens, her advice is to "do just one new thing."

I couldn't agree more. You never know where it might take you, not to mention the fact that it could get you excited about life, if you need a little boost. You can learn a skill you didn't know you could master or just have some plain old fun. And in the process, good things can come.

Step #6: Live Fully—It Enhances Your Appeal

Being single doesn't mean you can't enjoy your life. In fact, it's when you're doing that very thing that your MRM is most likely to appear. It may feel like the odds are against you, but it's not true. Life can be wonderful. Take a class. Go on a trip. Treat yourself to a massage. Read a good book. Sip a latte in Starbucks. Grab your camera and take nature photos. Spend time in your local library. Sign up for sailing lessons. Tune in to *Oprah* for some inspiration. The sky's the limit! Having a well-rounded life, including some spiritual pursuits, without a doubt enhances your appeal. Negativity is an immediate turnoff, and if you think it doesn't show, you're wrong. (Just think of all the negative people you know and how you and others feel about them.)

I hope that some of the stories you read in this book will help convince you that anything is possible and that strange things sometimes do happen. We could never in our wildest dreams predict them, so why not live as fully as you can right now?

Step #7: Act Like You Want to Get Married

Acting like you want to get married means having the mind-set to make it happen. You want to give people a chance, not overthink an opportunity, get the word out, accept fix-ups, make a concerted effort to get out of the house, and work on freeing yourself of emotional baggage.

You will do yourself a favor if you admit that perhaps, until today, you weren't really ready to meet someone, but now you are. This realization is vital, because once you see that, you won't get down on yourself for your efforts (or lack thereof) or the disappointing choices that have taken up your time and energy. The bottom-line is, you are now going to put yourself in a positive place—emotionally and physically—where true love is viable.

Boy Toys: Georgia's Story

One of my love-coaching clients, Georgia, says that the best advice I ever gave her pertained to her penchant for dating much younger guys who were emotionally unavailable. She recalls that I said to her that the young guys who interested her were "like a drug"—that, while they had fun on their dates, the relationships weren't real. They were a way for her to feel better about herself because they made her feel attractive and wanted. She was a striking redhead, but since she lacked some self-confidence, these young guys temporarily boosted her ego. Ultimately, though, they proved hurtful, because commitment was the farthest thing from their minds. They weren't mensches.

This is a really good example of someone's realizing that because of the wrong choices she made in men, she wasn't acting like she wanted to get married. Once Georgia was able to step back and examine her motivation, she was better able to admit that the men she'd dated hadn't been marriage material. If she truly hoped to walk down the aisle any day soon, she would have to better assess her dates and not be so flattered when someone asked her out. She deserved to meet her MRM but had to believe that for herself.

Going It Alone: Sharon's Story

I was speaking with a woman at the gym the other day. Sharon, forty-one, is an attractive, fit, bright professional woman, with an independent, active spirit. She has had her share of relationships in the past, but as we were sweating away on the elliptical machines one night, we had a frank conversation about dating. She discussed the challenges that she's been feeling of late in terms of attending social events or even a singles trip.

Though she has many single friends, for whatever reason, Sharon finds it hard to recruit someone to go with her to some of these activities. She and her friends have spent the past twenty years mostly meeting men at bars, clubs, and other random places, yet it hasn't worked out for them.

Sharon recently dated a man who was getting a divorce—or so he said. After they'd been going out for close to six months, he let it be known that his divorce wasn't happening so fast . . . and that, in fact, it might not happen at all. Sharon felt betrayed and has vowed to never again date a man who isn't totally available. She had put her faith in him and was completely wrong.

Looking back, Sharon knows that she could have changed her routine some time ago, but, instead, stayed on the same unsuccessful socializing course because it was the easy thing to do. No longer willing to be a creature of habit, she has been working hard to identify new outlets for socializing, and is excited at the prospect of doing different things, including weekend getaways, a cruise, and hiking trips.

Sharon learned that she has to take charge of her efforts and not wait for a girlfriend to accompany her. Going alone isn't her preference, but she's not going to let it hold her back. She is determined to make this the year that she meets her MRM.

Step #8: Assess a Relationship During Date Downtime

My friend Marla says that the most valuable dating advice I ever gave her, when we were both single, is that the way to evaluate a relationship is not just how you feel together but how you feel when you are apart—during date downtime.

She recalls being anxious and insecure when she was apart from certain guys during her single days, but didn't think much of it at the time. Looking back, it should have shown her that the relationships weren't meant to be. She herself admits that she wasted a lot of time.

If a relationship is progressing on the right path, you will feel secure between the dates and not find yourself in a state of analysis, trying to figure out your date's behavior. You also won't have to question if he has the mensch factor, because it will be evident to you through his behavior.

I can recall some of the men Marla dated—one in particular. He was very good-looking and would wine and dine her. They were always going to the hottest New York City restaurants and splashy parties. She was totally smitten and impressed, until his behavior became erratic. I was convinced, and even said to her at the time, that he was taking her to these places only because he needed someone to go with.

He did have a certain level of interest in her but, in actuality, would have likely found someone else to invite if she hadn't been available. He wasn't taking her to those places because he thought she'd enjoy them. In truth, he didn't do anything special to show his feelings for her. He did what he wanted to do, and she was basically along for the ride, as long as it was fun for both of them. She got to eat in trendy restaurants, something she enjoyed, but it didn't add up to much beyond that.

Marla felt the need to always look her best. She wasn't comfortable letting her guard down for even a minute . . . which is unnatural. It was further evidence that the relationship was not meant to be, because you shouldn't be feeling that this person will like you less if you don't look as perfect as possible. We all have good and bad days.

Eventually, Marla wised up and realized that he wasn't treating her like a true girlfriend. He showed no interest in meeting her friends or family and made no effort to introduce her to his. A mensch who is ready for commitment will want to make you fully a part of his life, and not just a Saturday night date.

So, yes, they were having fun, but it was more about convenience than anything. As soon as Marla started putting demands on him by being less available for last-minute invitations, the whole tune of the relationship, if you want to call it that, changed. You've heard the phrase "He's just not that into you"—well, here's a prime example for you. What does it take to realize that you deserve so much more? If you don't believe that, then that could be the reason right there that you're single.

Another gal I know, Sharon, whom I mentioned earlier, in addition to seeing how she feels between dates, has a three- and six-month rule of dating. She likes to reassess the relationship after she's dated those lengths of time to see how she feels, how the guy feels, if it has potential, etc. It was her mother who actually made this suggestion to her, and it's a good one. You don't want to spend too much time with a guy if he's not a marriage candidate for you. This is especially true if you question in any way his "menschworthiness."

GOOD ATTRACTS GOOD (WHEN YOU'RE READY FOR IT): ATHENA AND JAKE

Athena and Jake met at a writers' conference in Riverton, Wyoming, and had barely said two words to each other when he touched a nerve. He asked her where she lived, and she said she had recently moved to Wyoming to settle down after thirteen years of living in New York City. His response was, "If you were settling down, you'd be getting married and having kids."

She was so stunned—it was like he had tapped into her very soul. Little did he know she'd had countless failed relationships, including a ten-year one that never led to marriage or children.

They never spoke another word until the end of the conference. Earlier, Athena had seen him hanging out with another woman, so at that point, she felt she couldn't intrude. Despite that, she was compelled to grab her business card and set out to find him again, convinced that she had to make contact once more before she left. When she couldn't locate him, she stood there feeling devastated, like she had missed a "once-in-a-lifetime opportunity." At that moment, she looked up to see him holding out his business card to her and saying, "I've been looking for you everywhere."

Athena said she would e-mail him, and six months and thousands of e-mails later, he moved to Wyoming from Montana to be with her. According to Athena, to this day, Jake has at least a dozen binders with printed copies of their e-mails.

Athena explains, "After dating a very controlling guy for ten years, I wound up going for younger, commitment-averse men who were very attractive and fun but not marriage material. My husband was the first man I ever dated who was a straight arrow a genuinely nice guy from a small town. Ten years ago, I never would have gone for a man like him. I would not have felt worthy of him. Today, he is exactly what I want and need in my life.

"I thought marriage would be the ruin of a good relationship. I was convinced we'd bring emotional baggage and preconceived notions to it and both be tremendously disappointed. Instead, it is such a natural bond between us that I often actually forget I'm married and then remember that I am, and it is an incredible and amazing surprise to me. I think that waiting until I was turning forty was smart. I do not take our marriage for granted; I do not take him for granted. I know how lucky we both are to have each other. Marriage now gives me such a comforting feeling. I feel safe and secure with him and being married to him.

"Despite my suggesting twice that we get married, we ultimately eloped, and it was a mutual decision. To this day, after two years of marriage, he still tells me that he often thinks that he wants to ask me to marry him, even though we are already married."

MORAL OF THE STORY

It's never too late to make a true love connection with your mensch. Athena might easily have gotten so down on herself for spending years in loser relationships. Instead, she trusted her gut at the time she met Jake, and the rest is history. The point is that things don't always happen as we expect them to. If she were to predict her life, Athena might have thought that she would have gotten married long ago, but then she wouldn't be married to Jake. If we could write our own life stories, it would be easy to want things to play out a certain way; but if we believe in a higher power, we know that we are each charted for a course that we are meant to follow. Sometimes only with time, experience, and learning to trust your instincts, as Athena did when she looked for Jake, do we learn what we need to know so we can make the decisions that will truly serve us in our lives . . . like marrying a mensch.

Step #9: Be a Savvy and Strategic Socializer

I was speaking with a woman in my networking group the other day, and when I told her I was working on this book, she shared some of her dating experiences. A striking woman in her forties, she admitted that she had spent a lot of time going to happy hours and now realized that wasn't the way to go. She said that she wanted to meet a man of a certain means and sense of daring, and plans to take some weekends away and engage in other activities, such as fund-raisers, where she might meet them. In the past, she enjoyed dating around and admits that she might even have passed on a mensch or two because the timing wasn't right.

We also spoke about friends of hers and their dating styles. She mentioned that a number of them talk about having a "dating quota" for the month. What this means is that they consider themselves active socializers if they go on a certain number of dates each month. It's not important that the men be true romantic prospects. In some cases, in fact, they were just happy that the man treated them to a nice dinner in a fine restaurant. They knew they weren't looking to date him but took advantage of the opportunity.

If this is your approach, you are kidding yourself. So what if you have tons of dates each month? If you're not going out with mensches, you are wasting precious time.

Think about your socializing choices. Are you putting yourself where you're more likely to meet a mensch? If not, you're not being strategic. "Strategic" means you're not just going out randomly. You put a good deal of thought into the activities that occupy your time and, ideally, you will go where you're likely to find the opposite sex in numbers, so you have more to pick from.

DATING ETIQUETTE

- Does he pick you up on time? The date should be important enough to him that he gets there on time.
- Does he hold the door for you and pull out your chair? A mensch knows how to be chivalrous.
- Does he keep his cell phone on during the date and answer it? This is plain rude. He's there to focus on you. Who is he talking to? Prospective dates?
- Does he compliment you? He should know how to make you feel good about yourself.
- Does he eat like a barbarian? (You know—talking with food in his mouth and shoveling his food.) You will have to teach him table manners.

PHYSICAL GESTURES

- Does he keep his hand on the back of your neck when you walk in down the street? This could be the sign of someone controlling.
- Does he try to hold your hand on the first date? This is prematurely touchy-feely, in my book.
- Does he offer to walk you home or to your door? A mensch would be concerned for your welfare and safe return.
- Does he turn your lips toward his at the end of the date, when you have clearly offered your cheek for a kiss? He may be hard up.
- Does he eye you up and down when you greet him at the door? Animal attraction is great, but you're not a piece of meat.

- Is he up on current events? Ideally, you want someone with some smarts and an awareness of, or at least curiosity about, the world.
- Does it feel like you're on a job interview when you date? It's good if he asks questions about you, but it shouldn't feel like you're being grilled.
- Do you have difficulty thinking of things to talk about? Marriage can be for a long time, and you want to be able to communicate with ease.
- Does he talk on and on, without coming up for air? He's either nervous or self-centered. Time will tell.
- Does he dwell on the negative, such as sickness and failed relationships? You're not his therapist, and who wants to live with a downbeat person? Life can be challenging enough.

LOOKS AND HEALTH

- Is he clean and well-groomed? No further elaboration is needed here.
- Does he get an annual physical and take care of himself? You don't want to feel responsible for someone's health from the get-go. He needs to take pride in his own well-being.
- Does he have a sense of style? It would be nice if he knew how to dress himself.
- Does he try to tell you what to wear? Constructive comments are one thing, but you don't want to be dictated to. Is he trying to change you against your will or make you his Barbie doll?
- Does he wear too much cologne? A little Drakkar or Polo can be sensuous, but too much of anything is overkill. This can be overcome and, in the scheme of things, isn't a huge concern.

LIFESTYLE AND ATTITUDE

- Do you want the same things out of life? Ideally, you can share a meaningful life purpose with someone.
- What is his attitude toward money? I bring this up because, no doubt, you would like to lead a certain lifestyle. Decide for yourself what that is, so you can weigh the importance of his earnings potential. And if someone has money, how is he about spending it? On you? On his parents? On flashy designer goods for himself?
- Is he a couch potato versus a get-up-and-go kinda guy? Either one is okay, as long as you're compatible.
- Does he have an abusive temperament? People are entitled to get mad now and then, but a mensch would never get violent and take out his physical anger on you.
- What is his idea of romance? Do you want someone who writes you love letters, buys flowers, and reads you poetry in bed? Know what you expect, so you don't get disappointed later.

INTERESTS

- Does he cook? If he doesn't and you don't, takeout will become your sustenance.
- Is he a television addict? There are other things in life besides the tube.
- Do you want someone who enjoys reading, so you can share books with him? If you are a voracious page-turner, this could be important to you.
- Does it bother you if he has season tickets to the Jets? If you hate football, he can go with his buddies, if that's agreeable to both of you.

- Is his idea of travel going to Florida on vacation every year? I have always appreciated someone with a curiosity about the world and seeing new places.

VIEWS ON FAMILY

- Do you both want to have children? This is a critical question. You need to be on the same page.
- If he has children from a previous marriage, is that okay with you (and vice versa)? Know where you stand before you get involved.
- Does he have a needy sibling whom he plans to have live with him? This could be a tough one, since you may not be comfortable entering into a caretaker situation.
- Does he have a good relationship with his parents? Is he open to meeting yours? Ideally, the answer to both is yes.
- Does he like to celebrate holidays, birthdays, etc., with family? Family tradition is great, but if you don't love to entertain, it could get tiring if he expects every occasion to be at your house.

BELIEF SYSTEM

- Do you share the same religion, and if not, is that important? This could affect how you raise your children and live on a daily basis.
- Is he spiritual, or at least tolerant of others' beliefs? If he makes fun of your meditation practice and it's vital to you, that is disrespectful.
- Does he believe that women are primarily meant to be homemakers? You have the right to pursue your passions. You are not here to serve him.

- Does he expect you to quit your job if you have a family?
  If you are agreeable to not working, that's fine, but it should
  be your choice, too, not a mandate.
- Is he open-minded toward people and their differences?
  You don't want to date someone who is prejudiced.
  A mensch would never have that attitude.

HABITS

- Does he crack his knuckles incessantly? That could be
  annoying to live with!
- Is he a chain-smoker? That could be challenging to live with.
- Does he drink regularly? That could be dangerous to live
  with.
- Does he frequently tell dirty jokes? It's great to have a sense
  of humor and share a laugh, but if you find his jokes
  offensive and he won't stop, you have a problem.
- Does he drink orange juice straight from the carton? Maybe
  he did that when he was a bachelor, but those days are over.

Closing Thoughts

I wish you all the best as you go forward. I hope that some of the points I've made in this book, and the stories I've told, will help you gain clarity over your own situation and provide the tools you need to move forward and find the mensch to fill your heart.

Remember that love is like a box of Cracker Jacks: You have to dive into the box, weed through the sugary popcorn, and pick out the nuts until you get to the prize. But, trust me, it's worth it!